It's not TOO LATE to Cry

Living beyond the pain Psalm 126:5

ESSIE L ALLEN

ISBN 978-1-64079-733-8 (Paperback)
ISBN 978-1-64079-734-5 (Digital)

Christian Faith Publishing, Inc.
296 Chestnut Street
Meadville, PA 16335
www.christianfaithpublishing.com

Printed in the United States of America

Contents

They that sow in tears shall reap in joy.

—Psalm 126:5 (KJV)

Cry
verb \ˈkrī\

  : A jubilant sound that is made when you realize that you can
   have the life that God promised you.
  : To proclaim victory in Jesus Christ.
  : To make a decision to get back what the devil stole from you.

(Definition by Essie L. Allen)

Introduction

I remember the day when the Lord spoke softly into my spirit, saying, "Tell your story." I battled with the thought of unraveling my painful memories and sharing the dark moments of my life. I had become the master of illusion as I hid my true feelings. I began to wonder how people would react if they knew the truth about me. Would I be isolated even more than I already felt? I had worked very hard on developing a persona that I was strong and secure; but in reality I was broken, damaged, and weak.

Not having any concept on how to change, I was living a double life. On one hand, I was the good Christian while on the other, I was living in turmoil. I had allowed my circumstances to sculpt out my existence and dictate how I would live my life. I continued to struggle with the concept of sharing my life's story. I began writing all types of poems, short stories, and even sermons, hoping that it would give me some satisfaction and even leverage. It was my way of negotiating with God, but this wasn't what he was asking from me. He was asking me to open up and share who I was, who I had become, and finally who I am in him.

Feeling a restlessness within me, the fear of being open and unguarded before others was terrifying. I tried to ignore the voice of God, but it continued to echo in my spirit, louder and louder. There would be no refuting his voice.

Hiding behind the work of the church still didn't drown out the lingering sound of God's instruction to "Tell your story." God had spoken, and he wasn't going to let go that easily. My life had taken on the characteristics of that of Martha, Lazarus's sister (Luke 10:40). I thought that if I just remained busy, God would leave me alone. It was just another way of hiding. I had hoped that this would distract God from his request.

The sound of his voice was secure in my spirit. I couldn't escape. I rationalized that God must have made a mistake, that he couldn't be asking me to expose my demons. I would be placing myself in a vulnerable state, open to more pain and judgment. If he wanted a story, I could have suggested so many other people whose lives were more interesting. Still, I continued to hear the voice of God saying, "Tell your story." It was unyielding.

I didn't grow up with the perfect family, and my life wasn't a fairy tale. I would have to relive the pain and shame page by page, and this was too frightening to conceive. As I wrestled with the thoughts, I remembered the words in Matthew 19:26, which says, "With men this is impossible; but with God *all things* are *possible*" (italics mine). I gathered then that if I would just say yes, God would make it possible.

As I pondered on those words, my spirit became more pliable and the idea of sharing my story less frightening. The more I tried to silence the voice of God, the more it became clear to me that God saw more in me and was willing to use my life as a testimony for others. In that moment, I wondered what my life would look like if I dared to trust God. Finally, I said yes.

When I began to write this book, I was asked numerous questions, but there were two that resonated with me: "Why would you write a book that opens your life up to criticism and judgment?" and "Why now?" One word can answer both questions—*obedience*. God's Word is true, and I believe that obedience is better than sacrifice (1 Sam. 15:22). I could have ignored God's voice and continued to live the same way; but by sharing my story, God has given me freedom, joy, and the abundant life (John 10:10) that I longed to experience. I pray that when you read through the pages of my life you will find nourishment that feeds your spirit into wellness (Prov. 10:21).

INTRODUCTION

We all have a place where we find comfort and safety, and for me it's Sunday morning service. It's my haven of hope. I liked the fact that the service was orchestrated in an orderly fashion, except for the occasional praise break. I knew when to stand, sit, sing, and pray. I could hide in the open yet be unseen. No one questioned if you cried or smiled; it was all acceptable. There were also times in the service when the atmosphere became a tranquil oasis as we all welcomed the presence of God. I could feel his touch as though he was standing right next to me, making everyone's hearts beat in synchronized rhythm and my soul dance. I longed for those brief moments of connection.

My experiences had caused me to build a wall of protection that was impenetrable to the human touch. My relationships were superficial. No one was coming in, and I wasn't venturing out. I had become accustomed to living in isolation, even among crowds. But when you have a destiny, there is no hiding. God will use every facet of your life to reveal his power and purpose. Even when you don't understand the details of your life, God has a perfect plan (Jer. 29:11).

As I look back over my life, I realize that each situation and circumstance came with life lessons. Once I began to examine each part of my life, I was able to filter through the mess to find my ministry. Throughout the pages of this book, you will find some of my life lessons and what I've gained from each situation. I pray that with each lesson you will know *without a doubt* that God doesn't waste a moment of our lives, but rather he uses every single one to manifest his power; and through his power we become the people he has called us to be. You will also be challenged to find your life lesson through each page.

The overall lesson I learned was that God's love for me is the greatest source for living a great life. If you are living the life you always imagined, then you are living too small. Start imagining the life God has planned for you!

Chapter 1

Go Ahead and Cry

It was a Sunday morning; and I was in a familiar place, surrounded by familiar people and feeling the safety of predictability. The bulletin was the script that kept everything in order. After the praise service, it would be time for the opening prayer. This prayer set the atmosphere for the rest of the service. It had the ability to summon all the saints into one accord and remind everyone gathered of the reason for coming together.

This Sunday, Minister Jones led the congregation in prayer. He was a man who loved the Lord and took his responsibilities seriously. Minister Jones was a tall and burly man whose body towered over the pulpit. His very presence demanded attention, so as he walked to the front, all heads turned. It was as if everyone felt a sense of school days when the teacher demands your full attention. His eyes had the ability to scan across the congregation and pull out the troubles that may have been hidden. If the eyes are the windows to the soul, then his soul revealed that he was compassionate and concerned.

Silence filled the room in anticipation for this man of God to speak. He was God's mouthpiece. Minister Jones always cleared his throat two times—the first was to inform that he was preparing to pray, and the second was to clear the pathway so that his words could easily flow from his heart through his mouth; it was like cool waters quenching the dry places of our souls. He opened his mouth, and with a commanding voice, he said a simple but powerful prayer that invited the presence of God.

Heavenly Father, we come to you this morning, honoring you with our worship, knowing that you seek out those who worship you. So we thank you for your presence here this morning, and since you are here, we will revere your presence with a collective "Hallelujah!" We boldly come to your throne of grace with humble hearts, trusting that you are a loving father who cares about his children. You are a God who keeps his promises; and by your Word we are saved, healed, and delivered. Thank you, Jesus! Your grace is sufficient for us; and no matter what we might face, as long as we have you, we have the *victory!* Thank you for all that you have done for us. Let us surrender completely to your will so that we can be the vessels you called us to be. God, we love and honor you. Please have your way in this service. In Jesus's name, Amen.

When the prayer ended, the saints followed with a robust praise and a shared "Amen." Somehow in his modest prayer, we were able to hear from God.

Reaching back into our seats, we immediately grabbed our bulletins. It was time to sing the morning hymn, "Amazing Grace." I had sung this song hundreds of times before, but somehow following along in the hymnal always made me feel that I was a part of something bigger than myself.

As the words began to flow from my mouth, tears began to form in my eyes. Unaware of the cause, I dabbed my eyes with a tissue and kept singing; but the more I sang, the more uncontrollable tears flowed until I was drenched. The song had ended, and we were all prompted to be seated. But there I stood firm, unable to move. My body refused to return to what I perceived as normal.

A team of ushers came prepared to give comfort through tissues and fans, but after a few minutes, they were being signaled by the head usher to sit me down. Six pairs of the white gloves couldn't move me. My feet were somehow attached to the floor. Like a statue,

I stood there silently crying, afraid that I would drown in my own tears. I was troubled and uncomfortable with the changes that were taking place. God had interrupted my normal. God was determined to get my attention.

There was a woman who sat on the left side of the balcony. You could find her there every Sunday morning. I wasn't the only one who thrived on the familiar. From her position, she had the full view of the congregation, which gave her the duty of guarding the sanctity of the church. She was the eyes of God, and she was able to see me when no one else did. I believed that she felt an unction of the Holy Spirit to come to my aid. Quickly she moved from the balcony with such determination and power as though she was marching to the front lines to attend to a wounded soldier.

She was a spiritual medic, blocking and intercepting me before the team of ushers could take me down. Her words, although simple, had unlocked my frozen state. I followed her when she said, "Come with me." She reached for my hand and maneuvered me through the crowd of spectators. I had no idea what was going to happen next, but I was experiencing a willingness that I had never felt before. I trusted her.

I continued to follow her lead, my vision completely blurred by the tears. I turned to thank this woman, but as I walked up the steps to go to a quiet area, she was gone. I was unaware of the changing of guards. There I stood next to another woman I barely knew, but I felt absolutely safe. She took me by my hands and guided me to the floor. Once we were on the floor, she put her arms around me, and I heard her softly humming in my ear. It was just like a mama rocking her crying baby. "Go ahead and cry. It's been too long," she said.

Those words she spoke gave me freedom, unlocking the bottled-up emotions that I had refused to deal with I had been given permission to feel. Tears no longer represented weakness. The tidal waves of tears poured over me, breaking my internal barriers. This was the moment I realized that it wasn't too late to cry.

The transformation that had begun continued to unfold layer by layer until I was able to see what God sees in me. This woman simply shepherded me into the presence of God. The walls that I created to protect me from abuse and rejection were keeling over. My heart was now exposed, ready to be revived. I was longing for a touch from God.

The Life Lesson

From the beginning of time, God had been calling us back to him. He desires a relationship with us—a total commitment in which he can display his love, mercy, and grace. He wants to restore us. This is exhibited in the story of the prodigal son (Luke 15:11–24) who left the safety of his home and ventured out into the world. After he had experienced the degradation of society, he returned home.

With every situation I had encountered, I was allowing myself to move further away from God. Although I attended church, I wasn't allowing God full access to my heart, mind, and spirit. This is why it was so difficult for me to change—I was trying to fix my spiritual problems with worldly solutions. God will always welcome you back home, and as for me, my tears paved the pathway for me to reconnect with God.

The Parable of the Lost Son

Jesus continued: "There was a man who had two sons. The younger one said to his father, 'Father, give me my share of the estate.' So he divided his property between them.

"Not long after that, the younger son got together all he had, set off for a distant country and there squandered his wealth in wild living. After he had spent everything, there was a severe famine in that whole country, and he began to be in need. So he went and hired himself out to a citizen of that country, who sent him to his fields to feed pigs. He longed to fill his stomach with the pods that the pigs were eating, but no one gave him anything.

"When he came to his senses, he said, 'How many of my father's hired servants have food to spare, and here I am starving to death! I will set out and go back to my father and say to him: Father, I have sinned against heaven and against you. I am no longer worthy to be called your son; make me like one of your hired servants.' So he got up and went to his father.

"But while he was still a long way off, his father saw him and was filled with compassion for him; he ran to his son, threw his arms around him and kissed him.

"The son said to him, 'Father, I have sinned against heaven and against you. I am no longer worthy to be called your son.'

"But the father said to his servants, 'Quick! Bring the best robe and put it on him. Put a ring on his finger and sandals on his feet. Bring the fattened calf and kill it. Let's have a feast and celebrate. *For this son of mine was dead and is alive again; he was lost and is found.' So they began to celebrate.* (Luke 15:11–24, NIV; italics mine)

Life lesson question: What has pulled you away from the safety of your Heavenly Father?

_____

_____

_____

_____

_____

_____

_____

_____

_____

_____

_____

_____

Chapter 2

The Girl in the Red Dress

My story begins when I was six years old. Who could imagine that the best day would also be the worst day and had the ability to change the rest of my days?

Sundays were always noteworthy days in my life since childhood. I can remember people gathering in their finest of clothes and speaking like kings and queens. Everyone had a kind word to speak. People used Sundays as a time to replenish their minds and spirits. It was also the day that families would gather together and put aside disagreements in order to feast on love, laughter, and food. Sundays were good days. Or at least they were supposed to be good days.

It was the perfect day. The sun hung just above my head, shining directly into my soul. I could hear the birds chirping and see butterflies dancing as I sang my favorite song, "This Little Light of Mine." I couldn't ask for a better day.

My mommy brought me a new dress earlier in the week, and I couldn't wait to wear it. The excitement came because I believed that wearing this dress would gain me automatic entrance into the Big Girls Club. It was a red dress with a pleated bottom that continued to swing even after I stopped twirling. The top was draped with a white scalloped collar trimmed with yellow embroidered daisies equally positioned to catch every ray of sun. It was perfect. As I walked to the neighborhood church, I was welcomed by words such as "beautiful dress" and "she's a big girl now." The joy I felt was affirming.

Mom used to watch us walk to the church; and once we reached the door, she would wave and nod, signaling us to enter. This was Mama's only time to be alone. I didn't realize the importance of her alone time until I was an adult. Having those precious moments of independence, away from the demands of others, are so refreshing. After church, I would run back home to tell Mommy about everything I learned in Sunday school. Today I didn't run because I was escorted by my cousin who attended the church as well. He was my favorite cousin because he seemed so smart. I believed he knew God personally. Everyone said that he would grow up to be somebody important one day, and the fact that I knew him made me feel equally important. He was bigger than life to me.

Mom had an errand to run, so she left me in the care of my cousin. I was glad that he was going to be staying with me. He was so informative, and he could answer all my questions about Jesus. During the previous week, I had raised my hand when the Sunday schoolteacher asked, "Does anyone want Jesus to come into their hearts?" With both my hands raised high, I said yes, not really sure of the totality of my decision, but I knew Jesus now lived inside my heart. I was looking forward to learning all that I could about him. I was like a sponge. I wanted to hear everything about Jesus—what he did and how much he loved me.

When Mom asked my cousin to stay with me, he didn't hesitate. He responded, "Yes, I will stay with her until you come back." He was always helpful, so I wasn't surprised with his answer. We walked into the bedroom and sat on the bed. Everyone gathered there to socialize because that was the only room that had a television.

Before he had a chance to turn on the TV, I blurted out, "Tell me about Jesus!"

He stated, "What you do want know?"

"Everything!" I yelled. "How did he walk on water? Who were the men that were always with him? And tell me about Mary, his mother. Was she like my mommy?"

The questions ran so quickly out of my mouth that it sounded like one continuous sentence with no ending. "Wait a minute. Come closer and I will tell you about Jesus."

He pulled me close until I was on his lap. Then he did something I didn't understand. He laid me down on the bed. It wasn't bedtime, so I wondered, *Why is he putting me to bed? Is he about to read me a bedtime story?* Although I had those questions circling in my mind, I still trusted him. I followed his directions. I was caught unaware by what was to happen next.

He began rubbing himself. I thought that perhaps he had gotten bitten by a bug because his leg began to swell. There was a look in his eyes that I had never seen before. His eyes were dark and empty. *Where was the light that sparkled earlier?* He lowered himself on top of me, kissing my face and neck with such force that I was left with bruises. I couldn't speak. I was confused and terrified. Finally, he took his hand and touched in between my legs. The unfamiliar feeling caused my body to become paralyzed with fear. I laid stiff as a board until the loud sound of a door slamming caused him to leap to his feet. He ran from the room, the house, and my life for years to come. I was disheveled, bruised, and frightened; but no one said a word. I was left in silence.

I didn't know then, but I know now that I was protected that day. Because when all this was taking place, I felt myself watching from above. I was looking down on the man and the little girl in the red dress as though it was happening to someone else. My body was being destroyed, but my spirit was shielded.

The Life Lesson

For years I hated my cousin for what he had done to me. I blamed him for every bad relationship and every mistake I made in my life. I blamed him for the invisible sign I was forced to carry that made me feel worthless. It was all his fault.

But not so! It wasn't about my cousin and what he had done to me. What had happened to me was a direct attack from Satan. He just used my cousin to execute the plan to destroy my life.

> "The thief comes only to steal and kill and destroy; I have come that they may have life, and have it to the full." (John 10:10, NIV)
>
> For our struggle is not against flesh and blood, but against the rulers, against the authorities, against the powers of this dark world and against the spiritual forces of evil in the heavenly realms. (Eph. 6:12, NIV)

I was in a spiritual battle that God had already won. It wasn't until I grasped the fact that I am victorious through Christ Jesus that I began to see a change in my life. Everything I needed to move past and through this was given to me on the day I accepted Jesus Christ into my heart. What stops many of us from reaching our full potential is the inability to let go. I will share with you that the only way to truly let go is to change the direction of your reach.

> Brothers and sisters, I do not consider myself yet to have taken hold of it. But one thing I do: *Forgetting what is behind and straining toward what is ahead*, I press on toward the goal to win the prize for which God has called me heavenward in Christ Jesus. (Phil. 3:13–14, NIV)

Life lesson question: Do you know who caused the pain in your life?

_____

_____

_____

_____

_____

_____

_____

_____

_____

_____

_____

_____

_____

_____

Chapter 3

Daddy's Girl

Sigmund Freud wrote, "I cannot think of any need in childhood as strong as the need for a father's protection." A father and daughter's relationship can be the catalyst for how she will respond to all other men and how she views her own self-worth. He is supposed to make her feel safe and secure. He is her first glimpse of God.

My mother and father were never married, so he didn't live with us. But I could see his house from my kitchen window. I remember my mom saying that he was my dad, but a daddy-daughter bond had never formed. It was going to be a while before he even acknowledged that I was his daughter. He introduced me as "that woman's child" when others inquired about me.

The day he finally said that I was his daughter was when I showed up at the neighborhood store. My dad was already there, filling himself with his normal liquid spirits. I walked in unaware of what reaction I would get from him. The store owner saw my hesitation and asked my dad who I was. It was the first time I heard him say, "She is my daughter." I didn't know if I should be happy or sad because it took him to be drunk to tell somebody that I belonged to him. His acknowledgment didn't bridge the gap that I was feeling. I heard the words he spoke, but they lacked the authenticity of joy my heart longed to feel. I had watched enough television shows to recognize a real daddy, and he wasn't measuring up to the standard.

My mom believed it was important for me to know who my father was and to build a relationship with him. The responsibility of raising a child shouldn't fall on one parent only. She would take me over to his house to spend time with him, hoping that he would be the father I needed. I remember her dropping me off at the corner of the fence while he stood at the door waiting for me to come into the house. That short walk became the green mile for me. I counted each step. One, two, three, four . . . until I reached the gate door, slowly swinging it open. I began counting again. One, two, three, four . . . It was the exact number of steps from the beginning. No matter how many times I tried to change the steps, it was always the same number.

Only a few days had passed since the incident with my cousin, and it was time to go and see my dad. As usual, my mom walked me to the end of the fence while my dad stood at his door. I walked down the driveway, through the gate, and up the steps. I had begged my mom to let me stay home, but the words I cried didn't divulge my true desperation. The security I once felt was destroyed.

Being at his house wasn't like being with my mom. At his house, I would typically sit on the couch and watch television. He liked the old western movies and never let me watch what I wanted to watch. Basically, my needs were unimportant. Sometimes he would tell me I had to scratch his hair while he sat on the floor and drank a beer. I was treated like an indentured servant. I longed for the time I could go back home. I assumed that it would be the same routine as the other days: television, hair, and count the moments until I could go home.

But this time, after I walked through the door, I heard a loud bang followed by a click. This was the first time that he closed and *locked* the door. Then walking over to the curtains, he drew them closed. There I sat in the darkness, trying to follow his shadow with my eyes. I tried to watch his every movement. I was afraid.

Without a word, he slowly walked over to the couch where I was sitting and scooped me up in his arms. Through the darkness, he transported my small body into his bedroom. The blankets were scattered across the bed. It looks like he had never returned to his room since that morning. It smelled like an old musty basement smeared with old people lotions and cheap perfume. It was nauseating. The dust was thick in the air, making it hard to breath. *What's he planning? Why did he change the routine?*

It turned out to be a repeat performance as he followed the same movements as my cousin when he laid me on the bed. My body became stiff as a board; I was unable to move or speak. He sat beside me while his callous hands snagged against my clothes. He kept rubbing until he found a way to make contact with my flesh. He lifted me with one hand and began to undress me, tossing my clothes to the floor. There I lay on his bed naked, afraid, and ashamed.

How did he know what had happened? Was there something about me that screamed, "Touch her, use her, and abuse her"? Had I been marked for life? I prayed that a loud sound would come to stop him, but without a distraction, he took it a step further than my cousin. He lowered his pants, exposing himself. I wanted to close my eyes, but I was afraid of what he was planning to do. He positioned my body so that he could have total control. He looked at me as though I should have found some delight in this encounter, but the look of death is seldom happy.

His body covered me with darkness. Under the shadow of his weight, the light of hope was extinguished. After he had reached satisfaction, he took a dirty towel from the floor and wiped me off. With the roughness of his voice, he told me to get dressed.

As I began to walk out the room, I felt his hand pulling me back. I turned around and heard him say, "You better not tell your mom. I'll kill her." Those words framed our relationship, and for years to come, I learned to endure silently.

The Life Lesson

In my darkest days, I would remember the joy I felt when I raised my hand to ask Jesus into my heart. His love keeps me safe and brings me to a place of restoration, healing, and hope. I was able to find comfort in my Heavenly Father.

> [God said,] "I will be a Father to you, and you will be
> my sons and daughters . . ." (2 Cor. 6:18, NIV)

One Sunday, I heard this song by Chris Tomlin. This is the first verse (italics mine):

> Oh, I've heard a thousand stories
> Of what they think you're like
> But I've heard the tender whisper of love
> In the dead of night
> And you tell me that you're pleased
> And that I'm never alone
> You are a *good, good father*
> That's who you are

As my relationship with my Heavenly Father grows, I am consistently reminded that nothing in this world, past or present, will ever remove God's love from me. The more time I spend with God, the more I realize just how good he is to me; and those acts of my natural father can never outdo what my spiritual Father is doing in my life! Once again, the devil was trying to destroy me, but God's plan for me is greater.

> Trust in him at all times, you people; pour out your
> hearts to him, for God is our *refuge*. (Ps. 62:8, NIV;
> italics mine)

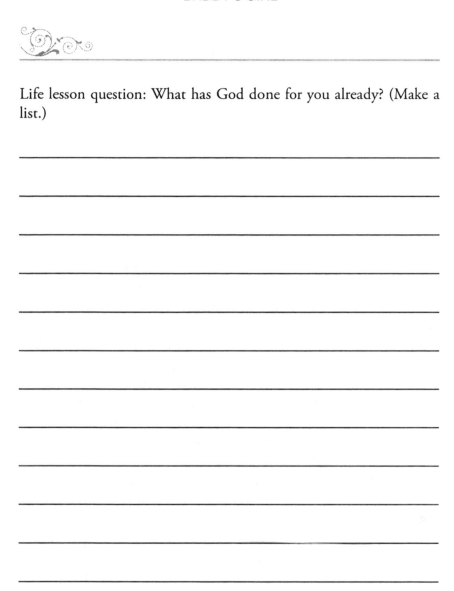

Life lesson question: What has God done for you already? (Make a list.)

_____

_____

_____

_____

_____

_____

_____

_____

_____

_____

_____

Chapter 4

Monsters in My Closet

My innocence no longer existed, and my ideas of love had been distorted. Forced to live by the cruelty of those who should have loved me, I felt lost and my identity crushed. Once a little girl with dreams, now living in a nightmare that felt like it was never going to end. Yes, there were monsters in my closet.

Innocence in the mind of a child is a precious commodity. It opens up unlimited possibilities, allowing children to dream big. It gives their lives hope and purpose. My dreams had changed from being a superhero, a ballerina, and a cowgirl. I stopped wishing for unending rainbows, dancing in the wind, and riding a horse named Cupcake. I just wished that I could go back to simply believing in those whimsical ideas; but the cruelty of others crushed my dreams, and wishing was no longer an option. I was thrust into a state of just trying to survive. My childhood was gone.

The one dream I held onto for the longest was to be an undertaker. This is a noble profession when you are an adult but rather creepy when you are a child. My fascination rested in the belief that they were able to find happiness in their obscurity. They could maneuver in and out of services without notice, and once their duties were completed, they just vanished as they waited for their next assignment. They became my superheroes. I wished that I too could just vanish away.

The safest place had become my bedroom. It was full of my things—toys, games, crayons—and there were no men. My mind became free to imagine, and I thought of ways to make this world a better and safer place for little girls. I thought about putting mommies in charge of the world. I thought about banning all men, except for Santa Claus and the Easter bunny. They were okay.

I would sit for hours by myself in the company of my stuffed animals. They were a captive audience. I would share my dreams with them without any worry of criticism. I spoke with authority and power. I was strong and determined. At least that was the impression I had gotten from my time with my dolls.

Because of the courage I felt from my toys, I made sure that I carried one with me all the time. Her name was Ellie. She was a beautiful lavender rabbit that my mom gave me for Easter. It didn't matter where I went; Ellie was right there with me. She became my protector against the monsters in my world. I had carried Ellie for years, and my security rested in her.

One day, my mom decided that it was time for me to stop carrying my stuffed rabbit. Ellie no longer looked like the perfect gift she once was. I had held Ellie so tight that she no longer resembled a beautiful Easter gift. Her fur was gone, and she had lost one of her ears and both of her eyes; but to me she was just as beautiful as the day I got her. She was now tattered with no hope of repair. I thought that if Mom could throw away Ellie because she was no longer new, what would happen to me if she knew that I was tattered and in need of repair?

Once Ellie was gone, nothing could take her place. I retreated inward as the fear of more abuse continued to prowl. My courage was gone. I regressed back into a shell—this time even thicker. Who could I trust to listen to my secrets? The time that I spent in my room increased. I was a little girl sinking into depression.

Once summer came, like most parents, my mother ordered me to go outside for fresh air. Reluctantly, I would go and sit on the front steps and watch the kids ride their bikes, skip rocks, or catch butterflies. My only connection with them was a slight smile and a hand wave. Nobody could know of the double life I was leading, and the fear of exposure hindered me from making normal friendships.

One day, I heard my mother calling me. She said, "It's nice outside. Go and play with your friends!" But I had no friends. *Couldn't she see that I was different? Didn't she know that I wasn't like the other kids and that nobody wanted to be the friend of the broken kid?*

I found my way to the porch and just sat and watched the kids play. While I was sitting on my porch, a neighborhood boy ventured into my world. He walked right up to me and began talking. Maybe he saw something different within me.

I wanted a friend. I wanted someone to remember who I was before the abuse. I was excited and petrified. My imagination ran wild. *Did he see beyond my hurt and pain? Or was he one who could see the invisible signs that were placed on me that said, "Touch her, use her, and abuse her"?*

I wanted to turn and run back into my house, but I remained. I took a chance on being normal. I listened as he talked about the things boys talked about—bikes, bugs, and boogers. He even made me laugh a few times. For a few moments, I felt normal.

When the conversation ended, he walked out of my yard. I assumed this brief encounter had ended until he turned around and yelled, "You can be my girlfriend. And on the first day of summer, I will take you to the Sand Wash, and do it to you!" I didn't understand the latter part of that statement, but it didn't give me a good feeling. *Did he like me or not? And what was he going to do to me? What was a Sand Wash?* I had so many questions but no one to answer them for me.

When I heard on the news that summer would be arriving in a few days, I looked for the boy who gave me the invitation to be his girlfriend. Once I saw him approaching, I yelled out, "I don't want to be your girlfriend!"

I still didn't know what he wanted to do with me, but I did find out about the Sand Wash. It was a dirt hole in the woods near my house where the neighboring company would dump its waste. I had already felt like trash, and now someone wanted to take me to a place where I could be thrown away. This just reinforced my belief that I was worthless and that no one could really care for me or love me.

The Life Lesson

I realized that the devil wanted to keep me alienated so that he could continue those private conversations of destruction. He wanted me to believe that I was the only one who was going through this situation. He magnified the horror in order to block my view of who I belonged to and who I am in God. He caused me to only see the bad things that had happened and transferred those views to everything that was happening.

Once I allowed God to clear my vision, I was able to see beyond the problems I had endured. I wasn't the only one; others had gone through similar situations and came out victorious, and so could I. The Bible tells us in Revelations 12:11 (NIV), "They triumphed over him by the blood of the Lamb and by the word of their testimony . . ." This is why it became so important for me to tell my story.

A second blessing came through the isolation I had endured. Do you remember when I said, "God doesn't waste a moment of your life?" During this difficult time of my life, God was training me to speak in public, think out of the box, write encouraging words, and even thrive in the area of drama. For a long time, I thought I lost my life, but in reality, I was gaining my best life.

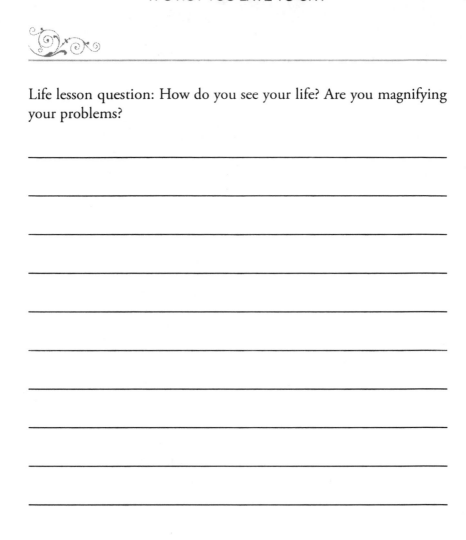

Life lesson question: How do you see your life? Are you magnifying your problems?

Chapter 5

Little Girl Insignificant

I was able to continue the masquerade throughout my adolescence. From the outside looking in, I was a normal happy little girl while inwardly I wrestled with feelings of sadness and shame. Could I continue this façade as I approached my teenage years? The awkwardness of high school would be my new platform, and the show had to continue. The venue had changed, but I was still wearing a costume that covered up the shame of that little girl.

My first year of high school was limited to one hallway. All the eighth graders were located in one area. When the bell rang, we resembled cattle being called as everyone jammed into the hallway. There was barely enough room to breathe. I didn't mind because I was able to hide behind those who towered over me. This allowed my small frame to maneuver through the hallway unseen. I was hopeful in my ability to feel invisible. That was until I was forced to leave the safety of the crowd.

Once a day, I was required to eat in the dreaded lunchroom. I was forced to mingle with the upper classmen. My only salvation was the good reputation of my older sister and brother who served as my guardian angels. I was off limits to the intimidations and pranks of the upper classmen. This was the one time I was glad that I was connected to someone else because no one bothered me.

The feeling of invisibility continued; and I was able to become a spectator, watching from the sidelines. Full of curiosity, I wondered, *Was I the only one? Could popularity, sports, or being a bookworm hide the secrets of the past? Did others share my pain? Did they have similar hopes—that someone would speak out, allowing the removal of the masks from our past catastrophes?* I wondered but I wasn't brave enough to be the first. A gesture of this magnitude needed someone stronger than me, someone who wasn't afraid to come out of the shadows.

The only gesture I could give was to finally join a club. This took all of my courage. I joined the Soul Searchers. It was a Christian Club that would meet weekly to pray and encourage one another. This was the perfect place for me to hide and feel free. My longing for God's presence continued to draw me into a place of assurance. No matter what I had to go through, the memory of giving my heart to Christ remained my continuous hope. I would often remind myself of the day that I raised my hand to accept Jesus Christ into my heart. It was a time of innocence and pure love.

When I first started attending Soul Searchers, I sat in the back of the room listening to others share their stories of God's goodness. Their words took me to a place where I could see God's blessings falling on everyone . . . just not me. Yet I still waited for God's undeniable presence, which gave me a sense of normalcy. In him my expectation rested.

Being a part of this group weakened my fortress to the point that someone was able to see between the cracks. *Had I allowed myself to become too comfortable in the midst of the prayers and encouraging words that I allowed my fortress to be compromised?* I must have done something that would cause a star athlete to notice me. It was the only explanation. He was tall, dark, and handsome—a chiseled god in his own right. He was bigger than life. His very presence could change the atmosphere just by walking into a room. Yet he saw me. A little girl. Insignificant.

There was something reassuring about the way he looked at me. His eyes were full of light. I was drawn in. *What was it about me? Could he see beyond the pain and isolation that carried my insecurities?* Whatever he saw in me, I desired to see it as well. I was

> It's funny how a stranger can come into your life one day and be your entire life the next day.
> —Essie Allen

34

opening up to feelings I had never experienced before, and I wanted to explore this newness.

Slowly we began to spend time together—simply sitting next to each other, smiling at each other from across the room, and the occasional walk home. The walks were always my favorite. It gave us time to talk, laugh, and enjoy each other's company. It was innocence. Love in its fullest. Finally, I was in the presence of a man who gave me wings and with whom I felt completely free. As our relationship progressed and the feelings became deeper, I had fallen in love and he became my entire life. He shaped the person I was becoming. It was a direct result of who he was: strong, smart, and beautiful. That gave me the courage to simply *be*. I couldn't ask for a better boyfriend.

We remained chaste for the better part of that first year, but the pressure was building. Feelings that should have never been awakened were wandering in my mind. *Could I call this true love if we had never made love?* Of course, my experiences were all distorted; yet I longed to know what real love felt like. He had to be the one. He was the only example I had of a tender and kind man. I made the choice. He walked me home, but this time, we were going all the way.

When it was over, I didn't know what to feel. I was confused. The voices that stole my childhood returned. I couldn't quiet them down. I became emotionally unstable: I loved him and hated him simultaneously. That little girl who was abused, broken, and ashamed, reappeared. I lost my confidence, my courage, and my sense of self-worth.

After our encounter, the relationship continued. He didn't throw me away! He really loved me, but I couldn't love myself. I felt dirty, used, and once again abused. It was nothing he did. It was the weight of my past that I continued to carry. I struggled to let it go, but it had become my foundation. So there I stood. The little girl in the red dress asking herself the question, "How could anyone really love me?" This was the first time that my insecurities caused me to doubt God's love. How could he love me when I couldn't even love myself?

The people in the club seemed so nice and willing to befriend me. There was another boy in the club whom I believed to be a friend. He would speak to me when he saw me in the hall. He went to a local church that I heard good things about. I took a chance on being friends. I wanted to trust people.

This boy knew I was in a relationship and knew my boyfriend well. They sang together in the school choir. Out of the blue, this boy asked me to go to his house. I didn't think anything of it. He wanted me to listen to him play the piano. He was gifted. Music was my second love, and I was honored to hear him play. After he played a few songs, he asked me if I wanted something to drink. I replied, "Yes, that would be nice."

He went to the kitchen and brought me a glass of water. He sat down next to me and began talking about his music and his dreams. I hung on every word. It was amazing to hear a young person talk about their lives so freely, engaging words describing dreams, a life desiring to be fulfilled. His future was being built one word at a time, laying a path to his future. I wished that I had plans for my future. I wished that I could speak eloquently of my dreams, hopes, and plans; but I was just trying to survive.

He moved closer to me as the conversation continued, and with one clumsy movement, he pushed me to the floor and laid himself on top of me. I couldn't speak. I couldn't move. It was happening again. He went from friend to foe. He fumbled against my body, and once he completed the task, I got up and walked home alone. No matter how hard I wanted to move beyond my past, it kept pulling me back.

I went to school the next day. I thought that the secret would be kept. But no. He wasn't like the others, who didn't want anyone to know what they were capable of doing. Instead, he went and bragged to his friends. Those hallowed halls of learning now echoed with the sounds of shame.

The story reached the ears of my boyfriend. We would always meet at his locker and walk to our classes together. As I approached his locker, the look of hatred said it all. He finally saw me through the eyes of disgust. I was worthless and once again alone. How could he leave me? Why couldn't he read between the lines of that story? It wasn't my fault! I never learned to fight for my life. I cried, "Please don't leave me! I need you!"

After what felt like a lifetime, he forgave me. His love was real and I was renewed. I made myself believe that he had the power to drown out the voices of my past. He was unaware of the magnitude of need I had for him without him knowing I had made him my entire life.

Getting back together brought on a new set of challenges. Although I was torn between my need to feel his love and the hatred I felt when I received it, we continued to share each other's bodies. No one ever told me of the emotional, physical, or psychological effects of intimacy. I was unaware of the changes in my own body. I associated the onset of vomiting with the flu. However, my mother noticed; and her instincts revealed the news before I even knew what had happened.

I was pregnant. The realization that a life was growing inside of me only came to my understanding when I was sitting in the coldness of a backroom. It was there when I heard the judgment and humiliation that was spoken over my life. It was my life, but no one asked me how I felt or what I wanted. With my voice still muzzled, the problem ended. I was no longer pregnant. It was a decision that would impact my life forever. I wanted to die. It was never spoken of again. It was to be another secret to keep, more pain to embrace.

On senior skip day, I took full advantage to spend the day with my boyfriend. There was something different about him. We hadn't been spending much time together since he started working. I called him that morning, hoping that he would be just as excited to see me as I was to see him. We went straight to his bedroom and began engaging in each other's company.

But there was no afterglow. Instead of allowing me to lay my head on his chest, he reached down to the side of his bed and grabbed a photo album. He opened it up and showed me a picture of him standing next to a beautiful woman. Her smile told me that she was more than just a friend. I looked at him and heard the words, "I'm going to marry her." It took a moment for me to digest those words, and when I did, I became instantly sick.

Without a warning, the earth fell from under my feet. Our relationship had ended for good. Things were never the same again for me. I fell into a deep depression. I couldn't eat and just wanted to sleep. My mom called it being "love sick." *Was there any medication to take because the pain was unbearable?* She told me that she understood the hurt I was feeling. I never questioned why she understood, but knowing that someone else knew brought me some comfort.

It took almost a year for me to stop feeling the effects of losing that relationship. I didn't know where to go or what to do from that point on in my life. I found myself all alone. I was going to have to reinvent myself.

The Life Lesson

Have you ever heard of someone who loves too much or too deeply? They become so attached to a person that their lives no longer exist because they have hidden themselves within that other person. They forget who they are, and they set aside their own dreams and aspirations. This type of relationship is unhealthy.

No one should have such a burden. I had made my boyfriend my god. Which in hindsight made no sense. He couldn't heal me. He couldn't help me. And he couldn't deliver me. He was just a man who needed the same God I served. It was God who created me, molded me, and designed me; and it is only God who can fashion me into the woman I am called to be.

And yet, O LORD, you are our Father. We are the clay, and you
are the potter. We all are formed by your hand. (Isa. 64:8, NLT)

So God *created* man in his own *image*, in the *image* of
God *created* them; male and female he *created* them.
(Gen. 1:27, NIV; italics mine)

And have put on the new man, which is renewed in knowledge
after the image of him that created him . . . (Col. 3:10, KJV)

Life lesson question: Where are you placing your affections?

_____

_____

_____

_____

_____

_____

_____

_____

_____

_____

_____

_____

_____

Chapter 6

On a Path of Self-Destruction

I was on a path of self-destruction. My pain had dictated how I was going to live my life, and for the next few years, my life took a downward spiral. I had relationship after relationship dodging the very idea of happiness. I was going through the motions in hope that my heart would follow, but it never did, with each relationship I became emptier. What I am sharing with you now are the results of my own decisions and attempts to fix my life without the power of God. When you are broken, the only decisions that should be made are the ones that lead you back to Christ.

Tremors are warning signs that an earthquake is coming. They signal the earth of impending dangers. When tremors are felt people go on alert. It gives them the opportunity to prepare for the awaited devastation. They find proper shelter, tie down items that might fall, and they make sure that their loved ones are protected. Up until now, my life had been a series of tremors. I prepared myself with isolation, I tied down my true emotions, and I kept the secrets of those who caused me pain.

The final tremor came in the form of a breakup. The earthquake of my life would soon follow. I was on a course of destruction that would affect all areas of my life, body, mind, and soul. The only precaution I took was to avoid any true feelings. I refused to pledge my love and devotion to anyone. I would not allow myself to be hurt again. It was foolish for me to think that way, but my heart became the real orator. The words it spoke pushed me to the edge, I had made a decision that I would never allow myself to feel pain again.

What came next was a performance worthy of a standing ovation. I was a one-woman show: "Lights, camera, and action!" I was on a mission just trying to survive, no one would ever capture my heart. The new attitude came with a new job. When I started working, I was required to spend most of my time in Atlantic City. The first guy to come on stage with me was Mahammad. We met at the Golden Nugget Casino where we both worked. It was a chance meeting that would have seemed magical if I didn't detest men. We always came to work at the same time, fifteen minutes early to beat the rush of the first shift clocking out. We would exchange pleasantries and go to our separate departments. He would always turn around and with a captivating smile, and say "After eight, we got a date." Meaning that after our shifts were over we would be back to the time clock.

I liked the attention, but my heart was frozen over. Those few moments we shared were enough for me. I found comfort in those mundane encounters knowing it would never be enough to stimulate the beating of my heart. When I didn't see him, it changed how I had to position my day. I would be forced to speak to other people and open up the possibility of new relationships. Interacting with him allowed me to avoid interacting with others.

After work, I would hurry to the bus stop so I could get a seat closer to the front. Atlantic City used Jitney Buses to transport. If they were painted yellow, they would resemble the short buses reserved for individuals with issues. I sat in the back once and felt like a smashed marshmallow in the bottom of the bag. Strangers having to sit so close that their bodies would end up being tangled together. I hated the thought of someone touching me.

I had planned to sprint to the bus stop so that I could get a seat up front. Before I could make a mad dash, Mahammad was waiting for me by the exit door. He surprised me when he asked if he could walk me home. I wasn't totally comfortable with that, but the alternative was less pleasing. Those Jitney buses were always crowded, and walking home would allow me to avoid the closeness of strangers. I felt at peace when I was outdoors. It reminded me of the vastness of

God and His unlimited power. When the wind blew, my imagination would allow me to believe that it was God's presence embracing me. It would take me back to those tranquil moments on a Sunday morning.

Mahammad was pleasing to the eye, his body looked like he was carved out of city stones, and his skin was like black silk. When he looked at me, I could see the tenderness of his soul. He had a rough exterior, but within him there was a treasure yet unfound. He was a diamond in the rough. His true value was hidden, but somehow, I was able to see the wealth of his spirit.

I felt a strong union forming between us. I looked forward to seeing him; he was the highlight of my day. Our time together increased; each week, rain or shine we would walk home together hand in hand. He felt like my covering. He enjoyed being with me, and although my feelings were unreliable, I found him favorable.

The closer we became, the more secrets he shared. Mahammad had a dark side; he too was living a double life. Besides being gainfully employed, he was also a drug dealer. This newfound information didn't deter me from seeing him. I was at a point in my life that I would rather deal with his dark side than face the uncertainty of my own heart. When we were together, we were able to escape the lives that we hated the most. I wasn't the only one who learned how to pretend.

I felt the closeness that we shared was pushing me back into a place I longed to escape. I knew once I got there, the only option for me would be to run. I couldn't take the risk. I let him go, before he had a chance to speak those three misleading words, "I LOVE YOU!" I saw the pain in his eyes; it was all too familiar. I knew that if I had stayed with him, I wouldn't be able to hide, he would eventually find out the truth "how I felt about myself." I was an adult feeling like that little girl who believed that "it must have been my fault" or "I was unworthy of anyone loving me." Those feelings surfaced to the top of my soul, forever leaking into my life.

I tried to stay inaccessible, but God's creative plan wouldn't allow me to be alone. No matter how much we try, we weren't created to live isolated lives. After a few months, I was in another relationship.

He was a good man, church going, hardworking, and respectful. He lived a simple life. I could be safe with him, but my mind wouldn't let me conceive the idea of completely giving myself to another. I knew that after a while, he would want to take the relationship to the next level.

I thought about leaving, but before I could call it off, he asked me to marry him. The proposal was so sincere that I accepted. I was torn between honoring him or taking a chance on feeling love. My fears won out. I looked for reasons to end the relationship, and when I couldn't find one, I devised a plan that would cause him to hate me as much as I hated myself. If he couldn't see the signs, I was going to point them out. I wasn't worthy of love. The plan worked, and just like Mahammad, he was gone.

My behavior became habitual. I couldn't commitment to anyone. I was living on a roller coaster. The ups and downs were making me sick. I wanted to stop, but my mind was so twisted that I couldn't recognize love when it was right in front of me. I treated God the same way. The fear of feeling any more pain was overwhelming. It consumed my total being. I wasn't getting close to anyone, and if I thought someone wanted to care for me, I would push them away, including God. Every time I would feel God pulling me closer, I would back away until I felt I was out of His reach. How could a God so pure and holy love a mess like me? All I knew about love was it caused pain. I kept God at a distance, the thought of Him turning his back on me was a pain too difficult to even imagine.

During one of my up moments, I met Bruce. There was an instant connection. Our time together brought me the "happily ever after" I desperately needed. His tenderness was able to reach down into my brokenness, touching each piece. He restored that fragile little girl and escorted her into the woman she always wished to be. He was my friend, my source, and my breath. Nothing could take that away from me, not even when he enlisted in the service. His love continued to reached me through the letters he wrote. Between each line, I felt the intent of his heart—it was to simply love me. Finally, I was in love, and it was real. Until I opened the door, that allowed the broken, frightened, abused little girl to walk back into my life. I began to accuse him of infidelity that was based on my own insecurities. I was afraid of losing him and how he made me feel. My fears directed my actions. "Get out before I get hurt." My mind told me it would be better to be alone than to risk losing my one true love. He gave me time to get myself together; his love was ready to take on the challenge to make our relationship better. I presumed the silence was rejection. I couldn't handle not hearing his voice, seeing his face, or reading his letters. I just let go. Bruce called me a few weeks later, but by then, I had moved on. The thoughts that I was unworthy had resurfaced.

I never really got over Bruce. I tried to find those similar feelings in another relationship. I was working in Vineland, New Jersey, when I met a man from New York. He had recently moved to the area after being released from a drug rehabilitation program. We worked together in the Industrial Park. He had a way with the ladies. Perhaps it was the muscle shirts he wore that exposed his well-built body or the way he walked that spoke, "I am edgy and in control." I found him alluring and was flattered when he flirted with me. I would catch him watching my clumsy persona as I dropped work materials, backed up the lines, and cried all the time. This was the realization that factory work was not my calling. He would laugh then come over to help. We spent our lunch time together, talking about his new life, hopes, and dreams. We were married in seven days.

I thought he would be my liberator. The knight in shining armor who came to rescue the damsel in distress. Once we got married, I realized that my life with my husband wouldn't be a fairy tale. It didn't take long before the demons he carried would surface. He was eleven years my senior. Instead of being my husband, he took the position of an authoritative father dictating my every move. He told me what to wear, where to go, and what to do. I was a wife living the life of a child. When my family would come to visit, he watched and listened to every word; and if he didn't like what was said, I could expect consequences.

I realized that the one thing I was running from, I ran right into: another abusive relationship. One day we had gotten into a big fight; he destroyed the house, knocked things off the wall. He threw lamps and vases and turned over furniture. Something within told me I wasn't going to live another moment in this environment. I was fed up. I began to pray fervently and call out to God. The atmosphere changed; the power was now in my hands. There was a calming in the air. After everything was back to normal, he said, "Don't you ever do that again."

My response was, "You fight your way, and I will fight my way."

We could never move past our problems to save the marriage. Four years of a tumultuous relationship had ended. I moved out and back home. I felt like a failure. How was I going to get past this relationship? I was now divorced, and God hates divorce. I was wondering if He hated me too.

The Life Lesson

> The Lord himself goes before you and will be with
> you; he will never leave you nor forsake you. Do not
> be afraid; do not be discouraged. (Deut. 31:8)

God hadn't left me. He was still there waiting for me to come
back to Him. He had been giving me signs to follow, that would lead
me back to Him. I continued to focus on the sign that read, Wrong
Way. It wasn't until I made a choice to follow down the right road to
my destiny that I was able to see my life from a different view.

Life lesson question: What voices are you allowing to give you
directions?

_____

_____

_____

_____

_____

_____

_____

_____

Chapter 7

The Devil Found Me in the Church

I went back to working diligently in the church. This newfound revelation was closing the gaps of my broken heart. The more I worked, the less I felt the emptiness. The transition wasn't easy. The awkwardness I felt in high school returned. You were expected to become involved within a group, and that group would reaffirm your identity or at least it would confirm what people thought of you. I was a woman, and I was single; my options were limited. I joined the women's ministry and the singles' ministry.

Out of the two, I enjoyed the women's ministry the most. We kept so busy that no one had time to really see me, no one noticed my struggles. I was able to hide behind the church clothes and slogans. All I had to say was, "I'm blessed and highly favored" to fit in.

The singles' ministry was the most difficult for me. It felt like more of a requirement than an option. The spotlight of not being in a relationship was always on. The older married women in the church would say things like "You ain't met nobody yet?" "What's wrong with you?" Or worst of all, "You don't like men?" I wanted to answer, "NO!", "NOTHING!" and "WHY SHOULD I LIKE MEN WHEN ALL THEY DO IS HURT ME AND ABUSE ME!" Church etiquette wouldn't allow me, so I would smile and say, "I'm waiting for the Lord."

While I was waiting, someone was watching me, and his name was Anthony. Anthony was a man of God who was swiftly moving up in the ranks of ministry. He was an acceptable match for several of the single sisters, but he chose me. We began to hang out together at all of the church functions. He picked me up for Bible study and sat with me in church. This was the true sign that we were together. He even stood in front of the church and announced that I was going to be his wife and thanked God for bringing me into his life. I just smiled because I didn't know how to feel. I had been let down so many times before, could this be the real thing? My walls hadn't completely come down, and I was still dealing with some issues of trust and insecurities.

As our relationship progressed, so did our time together. I would stay with him for days at a time, which caused us to experience a level of intimacy that was designed for marriage. We never shared this part of our relationship with the church. In their eyes, we were doing things right. I believed that this was the downfall of our relationship because once we slept together, those feelings of hatred returned. Even though we were going to be married, we were supposed to wait. It is God's mandate.

The more we became intimate, the more I became withdrawn. The very thought of him touching me caused me to violently shake and curl up in the corner of the room. It was too much for him to handle. What should have brought us together was tearing us apart. He decided to end the relationship and started dating another woman immediately. I was forced to watch her take my place; he showed up with her to all of the church functions. He took her to Bible study. The demise of our relationship caused the church to take sides. Instead of the church providing a place of healing, it became another source of pain for me. Playing hide-and-seek in the church didn't stop the devil from finding me.

The difficulties I felt made it hard for me to remain there. I made myself believe that everyone was against me. I even blamed myself, he was "perfect," and it was all "my fault." I wanted to leave, but through it all, I still needed God. I still needed my Sunday morning. I knew that if I left, it would take me even farther from God. I needed to stay connected. I was an expert at keeping secrets, and I wasn't going to let anyone know how much he hurt me. The walls came right back up. He was supposed to fight for me, he was supposed to love me, and he was supposed to be different.

I didn't officially leave the single's ministry. I just stopped going until it felt like I was no longer a part of the group. The women's ministry continued to be my solace. There is nothing more powerful than a group of women coming together to pray. We would lay prostrate on our faces, crying out to the Lord, praying in our heavenly language for the presence of God. His presence still brought me to a place of reassurance and comfort. Those brief moments would allow me to be covered in His grace when my spirit was heavy. Being in the women's ministry saved me from totally giving up, but it still wasn't enough for me.

My internal wall of protection was reinforced with every relationship I had encountered. This caused my relationship with God to waiver. I read in God's Word, James 1:8, "Their loyalty is divided between God and the world, and they are unstable in everything they do" (NLT). His word had come alive within me. I felt that I was going *nuts*. All of the areas of my life were being affected. I felt sick all the time, my emotions were all over the place, and my spirit was in disarray. I didn't know how to regain control of my life. I would pray at the altar, but the voices of defeat flooded my mind until I could no longer hear from God. Had He stopped listening to me? Where was I to go for help? Once again, I found myself seeking natural solutions for a spiritual problem. If God had given up on me, then I would take matters into my own hands. I made an appointment to go see my doctor.

Two days later, I walked into my doctor's office. I sat next to the entrance to avoid the other patients. I didn't want to waste any time with light banter. It was an emergency, and I needed to see the doctor now. When I heard my name being called, I jumped to my feet and quickly went into the examining room. I heard the doctor say, "Hello, how can I help you?"

I began telling him the symptoms I was experiencing. I was having trouble sleeping, I felt tired and lethargic all the time. My eating habits had changed. I was miserable.

Before I could tell him my entire story, he stopped me.

"Don't you go to church?"

I replied, "Yes."

He looked directly into my eyes and said "Your help is there."

I knew that even in my mess, God was still listening to me. Instead of the doctor prescribing drugs, He prescribed God.

The Life Lesson

Even when you can't see God's hands moving, trust that he is working behind the scenes. God can find you even when you are lost in your mess.

Life lesson question: What are you hiding behind? What are you using to medicate your problem?

_____

_____

_____

_____

_____

_____

_____

_____

Chapter 8

I Was Tired of Being Tired

I was emotionally exhausted. I was tired of being tired. How many relationships would I have to go through in order to find someone to love me? I was ready to just give up, and live a life of celibacy. Was it possible for me to be Baptist and a Nun? I don't know, but I was willing to try.

God has a way of being close to those whose hearts are broken. It's no wonder that I felt so close to Him; my heart was shattered. The whispering of God's voice always gave me hope. I could hear him saying, "Daughter, I have made you whole." Over and over again, my spirit was hushed at the beauty of those words. It was God speaking to me, His Words. I realized that God had been there the entire time. He never left me, He was waiting for me to respond.

I believed that my breakthrough came on that Sunday morning I described in chapter 1. The encounter brought me to a place of vulnerability that allowed me to be unveiled before God. I had begun a year of counseling, and this is a portion of what I experienced. Finally, someone would hear my story and validate the pain I was harboring.

There I stood, paralyzed, the emotional turmoil was overpowering, as the words of "Amazing Grace" pierced my very soul. I could no longer hide. I was a dam about to burst leaking from every side. Out of nowhere she came, one of the sisters from the church to escort me to a quiet room upstairs. There I lay in her arms until I was empty. I couldn't cry another tear. She was a woman who recognized my brokenness and led me back to the arms of God to be filled.

For the next year, I met with her, uncovering layer by layer the pain, shame, and guilt that covered my heart. I remember one session I had with her about forgiveness. She positioned two chairs facing each other in the room. She said, "You sit in one, God will be sitting in the other."

I had been avoiding having an in-depth conversation with God. He had become foreign to my heart, our relationship distant. I never imagined that God would want an audience with me. I followed her instructions and sat down.

What she said next startled me. She said, "Tell God how you feel."

How was I supposed to tell God anything? He is all knowing, all powerful, with all wisdom. He is God. I was hesitant; how do you begin a conversation with the Almighty? I began saying all the things I thought you would say to the Creator of the universe. It sounded right, but then she said, "Stop. Let the little girl talk to him."

Tears streamed down my face as I began speaking to God, "I am angry with you, you promised to protect me. I was only six years old, and you allowed those men to hurt me. I am broken because of you. I am worthless because of you. Nobody will love me because I can't even love myself. Why did you let this happen?"

I went on and on about how I was hurt and how I felt. I spoke things that I hadn't dared to think. But it was my turn to speak.

I was about to let God have a second round of my fierce tongue when, again, she said, "Stop. Tell God you are sorry, because He is sovereign."

Once I said the words "I am sorry, God," tears rushed out of my eyes again, and my heart was opened. I was ready to be filled, but this time, with the love of God.

She always had a way of asking odd questions that required you to search deep within, before giving an answer. This time, she asked me who was protecting me. I had assumed it was my responsibility to watch out for myself. So I said, "Me."

She then asked, "For how long?"

I blurted out, "Since I can remember."

"So you are the one watching out for you and you've been doing so since you were young?"

I thought I got it right, so with confidence, I nodded my head yes!

There was a brief silence, and then she proceeded to tell me a story about a war that was taking place far away. The tower was the center of the operation, and if the enemy was able to capture the tower, they would have won the war. Those in charge decided to place guards around the tower for protection. The guards took their responsibility seriously, knowing that the security of their troops rested in their ability to protect. Then she said, "How effective do you think the soldiers would be if they were required to be on watch for twenty-four hours a day, for seven days of week, four weeks in a month, and twelve months in a year?" It was an "aha moment." She said, "That is you, you have been on watch for so long that you are no longer effective. This is why you are so tired, and when you are tired, you don't think right. And when you don't think right, you don't act right. It's time you allow God to be the guard over your life."

My relationship with God grew deeper. I wanted to know Him. I wanted to understand how he could love me. As I was scattering the pieces of my heart; it was God who was picking them up. Shards of clay rested in the Potter's hand being shaped and molded into the woman of "I AM." Diligently, I studied God's word until it became the very substance that nourished my soul. I was changing; I could feel the scales of my heart drop away. New beginnings were on my horizon, and the view was breathtaking. My hope was restored, and I believed again.

The Life Lesson

The issues I had ran deep. I had been hurt so many times that I no longer trusted anyone, not even God. I had to be willing to allow God to be the protector of my life. I can't say that this happened overnight, but with time, inch by inch, I began to allow God back into my life, completely this time. My desire was for Him to reach down into the caverns of my heart and remove all the darkness I had held. Once again, I had to allow myself to be naked (spiritually); but this time, I would be trusting in God. The true protector of my life.

I will lift up mine eyes unto the hills, from whence cometh my help.

My help cometh from the Lord, which made heaven and earth.

He will not suffer thy foot to be moved: he that keepeth thee will not slumber.

Behold, he that keepeth Israel shall neither slumber nor sleep.

The Lord is thy keeper: the Lord is thy shade upon thy right hand.

The sun shall not smite thee by day, nor the moon by night.

The Lord shall preserve thee from all evil: he shall preserve thy soul.

The Lord shall preserve thy going out and thy coming in from this time forth, and even for evermore. (Ps. 121, KJV)

Life lesson question: What and who are you trusting?

_____

_____

_____

_____

_____

_____

_____

_____

_____

_____

_____

_____

Chapter 9

A Change Must Come

I needed a change. Although I had given up on believing in people, I hadn't given up on God. I wanted to find a place where God's presence resided, a true place of worship. Where the congregation was hungry for God. Maybe I was asking too much, was there such a place?

In my search, I found a small church in the woods. When I walked in, I knew that God was welcome. I found a seat and waited for the service to begin. The people were full of excitement. Their body language demonstrated that they were free to worship through song, dance, and the clapping of their hands. I loved to hear the choir sing because gospel music has a way of reaching down into the depths of your soul, but I needed to hear from the Lord. It had been some time since I felt his presence, and I was yearning for a connection.

In the midst of the high praise, the pastor walked up to the pulpit and began singing; his voice brought a calming presence in the church that made the transition from praise to preaching smooth. I instantly felt at home. The order of service matched my former church, but I knew I was in a different place. We stood together as he read the scripture, and as each word poured out, I was willing to open my heart.

I desperately wanted to hear from God. I listened closely, and I couldn't believe it—it felt like the pastor had taken an audience just with me. He knew exactly what I needed to hear. How could he see the brokenness that I had endured? Was my life transparent?

After church, I asked to speak with the pastor. We went into his office, and with tears in my eyes, I simply said, *"I belong here."* He didn't need a full explanation of why I felt that way; his response was "If God is telling you, then you are welcome."

This was a fresh start for me. My desire to want more in Christ led me to the one ministry I continued to love. I remembered the peace I found before, and I wanted to experience that again. It was difficult at first because relationships were already formed, and I was an outsider trying to find my place. My personality of being overly cautious slowed the process, but once I was in, I began to flourish. When it was time to reorganize the ministries within the church, I was approached about teaching a few classes for the women's ministry. I was overjoyed. This would be a time for me to connect with my sisters in the Lord and once again find the support I still needed. It would be my place of rest and restoration.

Even though my guard wasn't completely down, I had removed a few bricks, allowing myself to develop new relationships within the church. I was almost ready to drop the mask completely when I met Scott. He was truly different than any man I had met. He had strong family values and an impeccable work ethic. Whatever he put his mind to do, he gave it his all. He wasn't a complicated man; what he said, he meant. I didn't have to try and figure him out. He became a dear friend. We rode to church together and talked about the goodness of the Lord. Our relationship continued to develop. The foundation that we had built was spiritual, so I didn't have to be concerned about my wishy-washy emotions.

After a few months of riding to church, we went out on a date. He was the perfect gentleman. Scott loved the Lord, and it was apparent in every aspect of his life. He put God first. When we would hang out, he would always usher me into the presence of God by praying together, studying the Bible together, and worshipping together. Scott had standards and would not lower them for anyone, not even for the woman he loved. I respected him and said to myself, "This is how a woman is to supposed to be treated." I knew that this was the man that I could proudly see in my future.

We began taking Bible courses together. I was excited to see the growth in our lives together and as individuals. I thought he was just as happy as I was, but internally, he was dealing with his own issues. He wanted more for his life, and he even wanted more for me. By the time I met Scott, I had a good job, I owned my home, and I was driving a new car. He thought that he didn't have enough to offer me. He didn't have the material things, but what he had was greater. I couldn't get him to understand that the things I had were temporary but what he gave me made a lasting impression that changed my life.

Scott couldn't move past the fact that as a man of God, he needed to be in a position to offer more. He ended the relationship, and I was devastated. He preserved my virtue but crushed my heart. He wouldn't even maintain our friendship—everything stopped. It was an entire year before he shared the reasons why he ended our relationship so abruptly. Once he told me the reason, the level of respect that I had for him was heightened. He became the standard for what I looked for in a man.

I cried a lot during that year of not knowing. Again, I found myself in the same position. Attending church with a man who broke my heart. My pastor saw me crying alone one day and told me something that was both simple and profound. "He can't hurt you if don't allow him to hurt you." Those words became the off switch that stopped my tears from flowing.

I had the power to control my emotions? I had a choice? I didn't have to embrace the pain of losing him. The God I serve was greater. That was the last time I shed tears over him. I was taking my life back. I wasn't going to allow others to dictate how I felt. For the next five years, I literally ate, slept, and lived the word of God. Once again, it became the substance that sustained me.

I began to elevate in the ministry. My pastor confirmed what God was secretly telling me, that I would be ministering to His people. This was new for all of the women that were chosen to be licensed to preach the gospel. The pressure was great; I couldn't let down my pastor. I didn't want him to think that he had made a mistake with me. I couldn't let God down; He had entrusted me with such an incredible task.

I was more than excited to begin the ministerial classes. I was going to be learning from some of the greatest preachers in this area. They were going to share their knowledge and experiences with me. Each class brought me closer to understanding the person God created. Those classes had the ability to draw the hidden things to surface. Things that were buried beneath the ashes. Still, this new position wasn't enough. The fulfillment that I thought I would experience eluded me. There was no one to share in my new accomplishments. I tried to share how I was feeling, but the words never really came out right. The void and emptiness in my life was too vast to describe. When I said, "I'm lonely," it was ascribed to the fact that I didn't have a man. What I was feeling didn't come from not having a man in my life, but rather it came from my inability to connect with people, and it remained difficult because of the segregation that can occur in many churches.

It was almost impossible to develop relationships with people outside of your social arena. I didn't relate to the singles because at this point in my life, I didn't want to be in a relationship. Then on the other hand, I didn't have a spouse, so I couldn't hang out with the married women. It was an "old wives' tale" that single women corrupt married women. It should be called an "unwives" tale, because if corruption comes, it was already in the heart of that person. I wasn't trying to change anyone; I was trying to find a place to share my heart. I just needed a friend to trust. Someone who I could share my life with, without judgment or criticism. That one person who knew my pain and could love me through it. No matter how much I did within the church, I still felt incomplete, and I needed more. I worked without fulfilment, always craving for something more. Even though I didn't know exactly what I needed, I knew I needed more than what I had been offered.

The Life Lesson

I needed to allow others into my life, but who would befriend the broken little girl. Being alone didn't feel right anymore. God was stretching me so that my heart would be able to hold His love as well as the love of others.

> Two are better than one; because they have a good
> reward for their labour. For if they fall, the one will
> lift up his fellow: but woe to him that is alone when
> he falleth; for he hath not another to help him
> up. Again, if two lie together, then they have heat:
> but how can one be warm alone? And if one prevails
> against him, two shall withstand him; and a three-
> fold cord is not quickly broken. (Eccles. 4:9–12)

> A war that is fought
> alone is rarely won.
> —Essie Allen

Life lesson question: Whose keeping you company?

_____

_____

_____

_____

_____

_____

_____

_____

_____

_____

_____

_____

_____

Chapter 10

Broken and Blessed

S cott had become a distant memory. The bandages that covered my wounds were slowly unwrapping. It was becoming more and more difficult to keep up the masquerade. The pressure of being a preacher hindered me from getting the help I needed. Expectations followed the title. Who would have listened to a preacher who was overwhelmed with issues? I told myself that if I couldn't get it right, what hope did they have? This type of thinking gave me another reason to maintain my barriers and live in isolation.

I believed that if I would have opened up about the torment of my soul, all the work would have been undone. The many hours of service and sermons would have become null and void. Where can the preacher go when they are in trouble?

I was counseling others to work out their problems through the word of God, yet I couldn't fix my own. I felt defeated and automatically went back to what I knew best: living a double life. The chaos brought me comfort. I had learned how to master the elements of my darkness. The thoughts of functioning in any other arena left me incapacitated. Living totally free was a concept that escaped me. I was afraid of the change; who would I be if I wasn't the little girl in the red dress? I didn't know how to be anyone else. My hands were grasping to the end of my rope, and nothing could bring me relief.

I continued to bury myself in church and work, hoping that the situation would repair itself. The expectations of others fueled my need to continue with the facade. My life was out of control. I wanted things to end. I wanted the pain to cease. The only way that could happen was if I was no longer alive. I was a preacher who wanted to die; thoughts of suicide flooded my mind. The noise of ending it all spoke louder than the truth I held inside. There was greatness within me that I was unable to reach. I was broken and blessed.

Yes, I wanted to die, but my concern for others stopped me from ending it all. Even though my life was a mess, I felt responsible for other people. God was still using me to make an impact on others. If I had given up, it would have given them permission to give up as well. I couldn't take the chance that someone's blood would be on my hands and they would turn their back on God because of me.

I continued to suffer in silence. I was in a vulnerable place in my life, and the devil knew it. My personal time with God was slowly dissipating. I wanted to believe that He saw something in me better than I saw in myself. My obscured vision caused me to seek God even less. I was slowly giving up. The battle was strong in my mind.

How long was I supposed to keep up the act? I waited to see if I would experience another breakthrough that would lift me up and out of my despair. I wavered between the life I wanted and the life that I was living. I had given the devil an avenue to enter in, and this time, it would be even greater. I needed to fill the loneliness, so I began to work extra hours. I made myself believe that if I just kept busy, I wouldn't have the opportunity to go back and get into another relationship.

I was wrong; there was no place for me to hide. While at work, I met a man that piqued my curiosity. He was the strong and silent type. When he did speak, his conversation went beyond the mundane topics that were usually exchanged on second shift. He always had a nugget of wisdom to share.

Cautiously, I was drawn in; there was something so familiar about him. Caution moved toward connection, and before I knew it, we were sharing the bits and pieces of our lives. Our brokenness served as a balm for each other. We couldn't help ourselves, but we were able to give sound advice for each other's problem. You could say that he was the male version of myself, always ready to encourage someone else while self-help was impossible to find.

One day while working together, I volunteered to help him with dinner preparation. It was a simple dinner: chicken, rice, string beans, and buttered rolls, but the amount made it no simple task. Cooking for twenty people was time consuming. The kitchen was small and the pots and pans were army size. The sounds of cans opening and food being stirred in the pots was able to cover the closeness we shared. Our conversations became the perfect oasis; we were able to lose ourselves within each words. No one seem to notice that dinner was late that night. We had spent hours sharing our hopes and dreams. It felt like an outer-body experience with him. I saw the person I could become. His conversations made me alive. I made sure that I was on the schedule when he worked. Our talks were my lifeline. I could say things to him, that I wanted to share with God. He had become my friend, and I felt safe.

Just when I thought I found my connection, he was gone. He took another job, and I was left feeling more alone than I did before. The schedule was completed for the month, so there I was at work, thinking about him, wishing that he was thinking of me. His absences left a void in my heart.

Who would be the filler of my soul? I missed our conversations, but I continued to work extra hours, hoping that I would encounter another familiar soul. I didn't, but I did meet another guy named Carl. He was someone who liked to talk, and although his conversations weren't inspiring, it filled the void. Carl was always at work, and I could appreciate that because I spent most of my time working double shifts to avoid being alone. The silence I heard in my house echoed a consistent reminder that no one wanted to know the little girl in the red dress.

I liked his company. He was someone to talk to. Work became the simplest way to socialize without the pressure of building relationships. I wasn't concerned about becoming too close to Carl because our lives were so different. We were on two different paths without the possibility of crossing. Especially outside of work.

I don't know when it happened, but the conversations took us to a place that was too familiar to me. His advances were subtle. I never thought he could be interested in me. Our lives were like night and day. What we wanted and needed was different. He enjoyed the things of the world, and I was still the daughter of the King, even though I didn't always wear the royal crown. The instability of my emotions caused a battle within my spirit to hold strong.

Our conversations gradually spilled over into our private lives. After work, he would come over to my house to unwind. We would talk and laugh for hours. We became closer and closer until we shared more than words.

Yes, I found someone to connect with, but the connection was frayed. I tried to make myself believe that this would be enough for me. I kept our relationship a secret because I didn't want to hear the truth. We were unequally yoked, and he really didn't care about me.

I was setting myself up for failure. I just needed to feel like someone could care about me. I needed to feel a part of something outside of myself. I wanted to be wanted. We would meet for late-night rendezvous. Maybe it was the secrecy that made things feel so exciting, or the expectation that had built up throughout the day from stolen glances. Whatever it was, it was wrong, and it wouldn't last.

It wasn't all sex; we tried to engage in each other's company by going to concerts and plays, but there was something missing—a consistent disconnect. All this was just a temporary fix. It was like placing duct tape on a leaking pipe; sooner or later the pipes are going to need to be replaced. I needed something better, I needed to get out of this rut. I didn't know how to break the cycle, but God did. It was with three little words, "I am pregnant."

The look he gave me was as if I was speaking a foreign language. There would be no celebration. We were strangers that would be forever connected. I didn't want to believe it either how this had happened; this wasn't the plan. Was God giving me another chance? Did he forgive me for sitting in the darkness of that back room? No one was going to tell me what to do—it was my body, my life, and my choice. My life was about to take a swift turn, and I better be ready for the ride.

Before anyone could start the rumors, I went to work and let my staff know that I was going to have a baby. I figured if I told them first, it would stop the whispers. It didn't. There is always that one person who has to say something. Ms. Ritter came to me and asked "Who is the father?" My response was short and sweet, "None of your business."

My response didn't go over well with her; she went on a witch hunt to find out who was the father of my child. She asked everyone and even started rumors that got back to Carl. This didn't help. He was looking for any reason to abandon the truth. I had regretted that I kept the relationship a secret. I really needed him to stand up for me. I needed him to be my voice.

The time that we spent together became less and less until he was out of the picture altogether. The person that once brought me some happiness now hated me. I had access to his body, but his heart was far from me. He didn't plan on having another child, and the weight of that situation fell on me. Everything became my fault. It was my fault that he couldn't go back to school. It was my fault that he couldn't get out of debt. It was my fault that he had to work more hours. It was my fault that his dreams were deferred. I tried to ignore how he made me feel, but his attitude toward me caused a sense of hatred for him; he made me feel like that little girl who didn't have the power to fight for her life.

My life was changing too, but God made sure it would be for the better. My character was now in question. I was ashamed. The reality of my situation didn't leave me a choice. I had to deal with it. Remember when I said that there will be times when God works behind the scene in order to change your life? The pregnancy wasn't just a sign of my sin, but rather it was a sign of God's grace. He revealed me in order to heal me. Once again, God stepped in, orchestrating the healing I needed.

The Life Lesson

> It was good for me that, I have been afflicted; that
> I might learn thy statutes. (Ps. 119:71)

I could no longer hide. It was out and in the open. I was broken and struggling with issues that were bigger than me. I needed help, and God was going to make sure I got what I needed. Once again, I was left abandoned, but this time, I was willing to allow God to find me in my loneliness. God showed up even greater in my life. I had to depend on Him completely.

Life lesson question: What lessons are you learning from your issues?

_____

_____

_____

_____

_____

_____

_____

Chapter 11

New Beginnings Can Start Now

It was one thing to tell the people at my job, but my church was another story. The ministerial classes had finished, and I was about to become a licensed minister. I was overcome with shame and guilt. There were people who believed in me, counted on me, and took a risk on me. I had let them down. I had let God down. How do I get up from this? I never did find the courage to tell my church family. I just stopped coming to church.

I was crazy to think that they would never find out. It was a sunny day, and I happened to be sitting outside when my pastor's wife rode by my house. I couldn't hide fast enough. She turned the car around and came to where I was sitting. I thought that she was coming to reprimand me for my sinful ways. I couldn't be farther from the truth. She simply loved me. She was concerned about my health and well-being. She wanted me to know that I was missed, and she couldn't wait until I was back in fellowship. My shame and guilt were removed. I felt renewed.

A few weeks later, I got a call from my pastor, and his words brought restoration; he simply said, "When are you coming back?"

Those words made the walk of shame I had imagined turn into a walk of joy. Before I actually came back, I met with the pastor, and he spoke not only as a pastor but as a loving father. He gave me what I needed: affirmation.

His conversation released in me the power to do what God had called me to do: minister the gospel. I became active in many areas of service. God reassured me that He still wanted to use me for His glory.

I could no longer hide the issues that had caused me to struggle. My sin was fornication, but my issue ran deeper. Although I had gone through counseling, I didn't completely surrender to God. There were parts of my life I still didn't have the courage to face.

After an acceptable time, I was restored back into the ministry. I had to learn how to balance motherhood and all the requirements of a minister. I was grateful for this second chance, so I didn't complain.

I continued to attend ministerial classes, teach, and help out in the drama ministry. Things were going well. I was finally going to be licensed as a minister. It seemed like I waited a lifetime.

The day had finally come. All the ministers gathered in the pastor's office. As I sat there, I began to cry; the pastor thought it was my nerves, but I was in awe of God that He would continue to use me. I was humbled by His unconditional love, grace, and mercy he had for me.

As I walked into the sanctuary, it was full of people who had seen me fall but still believed in me. The order of service flowed just the way it does on a Sunday morning. The scripture and prayer were given followed by a few selections from the choirs. The presence of God had rested in this place, and I was ready to share what He had given me.

After my introduction, I walked up to the pulpit, opened my Bible, and read from Exodus. After I prayed, I began to tell the story of Moses from Exodus 17; one thing that stood out to me was in verse 12, "But Moses' hands were heavy; and they took a stone, and put it under him, and he sat thereon; and Aaron and Hur stayed up his hands, the one on the one side, and the other on the other side; and hands were steady until the going down of the sun." My key point was that when you are in the battle, it's okay to rely on others to help you fight.

The word of God was powerful and moved as I preached, but somewhere deep inside of me, I couldn't do what I had preached. I wasn't able to share my struggles. Even with this new beginning, I still felt feelings of isolation. The voices of defeat continued to speak in my mind. I couldn't articulate the stress I was experiencing, so I kept quiet. I refused to speak of it because who would have understood? I hoped that those feelings would eventually go away. I was wrong.

I would place all my focus on working the ministry and being a good mom. I thought things were going well, until I began to feel an uneasiness within my spirit. There was a question that continued to linger in my mind, "What is my purpose?"

For three years, I searched for the answers. I asked a fellow member, "What would you say is my purpose?"

Their responses were never able to completely answer the question. In some regard, they just pacified the question, by saying, "We need you here."

In my desperation, I even asked someone in the human resources department at my job, and her response was, "We need you here, you offer things," as she walked away to attend to more pressing issues. Not knowing who you are and what purpose you serve can cause you to feel a hollowness deep within.

No one could give me an answer. The lack of an answer allowed my mind to wander. "Why was I in church?" "Was I even important to the body of Christ?" and "What on earth was I doing here?" Those questions rang loud and were magnified through my inability to form healthy relationships. I had no one to contradict how I was feeling.

It was March 2012, and it was my turn to preach. The question that I had longed to be answered formed my sermon. There was something different about this morning. I couldn't put it into words. I felt a strength that seem to surround me. I felt guarded and powerful. I had prepared for weeks and was ready to burst. It was a word that hit home first. I was passionate about what God had shared with me.

> I still remember the message that I preached that morning.: *"That I may know him."*
>
> "That I may know him, and the power of his resurrections, and the fellowship of his sufferings, being made conformable unto his death" (Phil. 3:10, KJV).

My hunger had returned, and my desire was to know more about Jesus. I needed more than the church experience, I needed a personal encounter with Him. I had gotten so "churched" that I was missing out on knowing Him away from the order of religion.

After I had preached, I knew God had heard my cries. He was going to do something, even though I didn't know exactly what. I was opened and willing to experience what He had plan for me. I hadn't shared my most inner thoughts with anyone, but I wanted to leave the church. I wanted to move beyond what I had learned to be the church experience. Sunday morning services, choir rehearsals, prayer meetings, Bible studies, and meetings upon meetings. I felt stuck.

There was a brief break before the benediction, and I received word that my son had made a decision to leave this church. I was surprised, because at this time, he was only ten years old. He had resigned from the sound ministry and the junior ushers. When asked why he was quitting, he replied, "I'm going to my new church."

Once again, God had used a child to change the world. Well, my world at least. This was God's way of moving me into my destiny. I didn't tell the church that I was leaving, but rather, I said, "Since my son can't drive, I will be required to take him to his new church." Somehow, the truth got lost in my wording. I was leaving as well. This would be my last Sunday.

I was torn about the decision to leave. I had spent seventeen years with this church, and although I didn't feel loved, I knew that there were people there who loved me. The need to find out how I fit in the scheme of things was my driving factor. I wanted to know what God had for my life. I had to take a chance and move beyond the lines in the sand. I had to be willing to walk to the water and dive in. It was called living.

The Life Lesson

Even though my words couldn't speak the condition of my heart, God knew what I needed. He is the God of my past, God of my present, and God of my future. He caused a stirring in my spirit that wouldn't allow me to be content where I was physically, emotionally, and spiritually. He had more for me, and the only way I was going to experience the totality of who He is and who I am within was to change my position. Change is inevitable. It happens with or without our permission. I learned to allow God to be my guide through the change. I embraced the newness's in my life knowing that with each new level, I would get a closer look at my Savior.

Life lesson question: Do you really want to change?

> If we don't change, we don't grow. If we don't grow we aren't really living.
>
> —Gail Sheehy

_____

_____

_____

_____

_____

Chapter 12

I Am in the Wilderness

The desire to fill the emptiness was greater than my need to stay. It was the voice of a child that drew me out, and I found myself attending another church. It was a place that my family had frequented, but once I arrived, I felt like I was in the wilderness. My family had asked me to come to the Christmas fellowship, and I had no reason not to come. Eight months had passed, and no one from my former church had reached out to me. Maybe just leaving was enough. I was hurt that my absence didn't bother anyone. Maybe what I felt was true, I served no purpose. The devil magnified those feelings of rejection and abandonment. Once again, my mind had to battle with those negative thoughts.

I arrived at the church and automatically, I was greeted with warmth that was unfamiliar. I wasn't treated like a guest. I was treated like family—I mean the family member that you loved to see. The love that I received was overwhelming. This couldn't be true; people don't just love you like that, and there must have been another agenda. I didn't look like them, I didn't sound like them, but they loved me like I belonged. This left me with a feeling of uneasiness, but comfort.

I went back the next Sunday, and they invited me to hang out with some of the youth from church and their parents. We went to the movies and then out to dinner. It had been a long time since I had been out, and talking to adults was a rare occurrence. The conversation was tailored to getting to know me, not the position or titles I held. They wanted to get to know me. I held the joy I felt inside; they made me feel like I was a person worthy of being loved. I still wasn't ready to open up, so I didn't share too much about me. I geared the conversation to placing names with faces. Internally, I wondered what they would think if they knew the real me, the one who had struggles, the one who was afraid to allow people in, the one who was in some regards still broken.

I made myself believe that invisibility was my greatest strength. I would come to church, find God, and go home. I politely greeted people with those church slogans that informed others that you are no stranger to this church thing. My conversations were brief, and making eye contact wasn't an option. I didn't want someone to misconstrue that I wanted to talk. Until I realized that this church wouldn't allow me to keep to myself, they believed in fellowship. They weren't just going to leave me alone. I heard the pastor say one day that one of their greatest responsibilities was to love people like Jesus loved people. It was more than words they had actually taken on that mantel. It was common to hear someone say, "We are the hands and feet of Jesus." In other words, they were willing to do the work of Christ.

When I arrived at church this particular morning, I was overwhelmed by the circumstances of life. I was running late, I had my mother who was in a wheelchair, a friend's child, and my son. I walked through the doors with my painted smile and church slogans, "Good morning, and God bless you." A woman greeted me, and I tried to pretend that I was fine; she literally saw behind the mask I was wearing. She told me to stop, slow down, and breathe; God was in control. She made sure that the little hyper kid went to children's church; she took my mom to service and sat with her until I finished my class. I was able to breathe. This was God in action. I had been waiting to receive this upper room experience of God's presence when He was showing me Himself in the actions of others. I was able to see the love of God in ordinary people. The love that I was looking for was around me the entire time; my vision had been blocked by the thoughts I harbored from my past.

That one kind act opened my eyes to see the work of God. When people needed prayer, there was no, "I'll pray for you" and go on your way. They stopped and prayed for people at that moment. It wasn't a long, loud, or "I want people to see me" prayer. It was simply praying the word of God over their situation. I was mesmerized by the confidence they exhibited. They didn't allow anything to hinder the opportunity to share the love of God.

I started to think that I could never measure up with such deliberate acts of God. I was naturally guarded, although I had been in positions that required me to be out and up front. I was never completely secure in that environment. This lack of confidence hindered me from releasing the true power that God had given me. How was I going to fit into this new church?

When I think about how I was brought into the work of the ministry, the best way to describe it, is as a *push of faith*. I remember having a large slide at my son's birthday party. I had walked up to the top, and when I looked down. I told myself that I couldn't do this. I tried to turn around, but the person behind me gave me a push, and I had to follow through. (It didn't help that I would have looked like a wimp to the group of seven-year-olds that had already done it and succeeded.) Well, the church gave me a push. They didn't allow me to function in my fears. They showed me the importance of partnering with others. God's kingdom is too vast to work alone. I learned how to be the hands and feet of Christ. They allowed me to witness and participate in random acts of kindness that ushered people into the presence of God.

The powerhouse within began to slowly unfold. I began to invest in people, through numerous venues, visiting the elderly, cleaning up abandoned houses, volunteering at the food bank, collecting socks for the homeless, and sharing the word of God through drama and preaching. Since coming to this new church, I have been pushed beyond my own insecurities to trust God.

I was honored when the pastor asked me to share on a Sunday morning. I remember one particular time it was the *Christmas* Story from a woman's viewpoint. I had rehearsed and rehearsed, going over every line and scripture to portray Elizabeth and her encounter with

Mary the mother of Jesus. I wanted the congregation to understand the power of Jesus Christ that was unveiled before His birth. I had to minister for both services. The first service went well. I kept my notes close because I didn't think I could do it justice without the papers I held in my hands. As I sat in a quiet room, the pastor came to me and said, "It's in you, put the papers down."

Those words pushed me to release a greater anointing that was on my life. I was amazed that someone was able to see more in me. I was being pushed to become greater. Since those words, I have learned how to move past acceptable and reach for excellence. My life took another turn. I had someone who was invested in the greater me. Over the last few years, I have been able to see the move of God in my life. I can't go back to the isolated existence that I called my life. I am free.

That was only the beginning; through the various outreaches, I witnessed the miraculous love of God. I was being pushed out of my comfort zone. The isolation that I felt kept me safe was no longer a haven for me. Every day, God was showing me the unconditional love I so desperately wanted and needed. I was being awakened to the purpose and destiny that God had designed for me. I was changing in such a way that it almost seemed natural. It wasn't forced, it wasn't coerced, it was me walking step by step into the woman God knows I am. God was calling for more. The devil's lies couldn't stand. My life was a part of something bigger. My struggles were now empowering me.

The Life Lesson

> Being *confident* of this very thing, that he which hath *be*gun a good work in you will perform it until the day of Jesus Christ: (Phil. 1:6, emphasis mine)

I had always believed the Word of God for others, but now, my confidence rested in the Word of God for me. He said it and I believed it! Finally!

Life lesson question: Do you believe that you are worth changing?

_____

_____

_____

_____

_____

_____

_____

_____

Chapter 13

The Turnaround

When I gave my life to Christ, He had equipped me with everything I would need to live a successful life. I recognized that I had the power to change my situation, and once I believed that, I could see it manifested. Once my mind was renewed, I was able to imagine the possibilities that God had for me. The thought of change wasn't so terrifying. I longed to see a new and better life. I can't say that this change happened instantly, it would be over a span of time and allowing God to define my process. Step by step, I was able to reach a place in my life that I could take hold of the scriptures and apply them to my life and make a turnaround. Remember when I said that I believed God for everyone else? Now, I believed Him for me, the realization of His Word manifested in my life. Yes, I was isolated, rejected, and abandoned, but those situations brought me to a better understanding of who I am in Christ.

> That the trial of your faith, being much more precious than of *gold* that perisheth, though it be tried with *fire*, might be found unto praise and honour and glory at the appearing of Jesus Christ: (1 Pet. 1:7, KJV; emphasis mine)

I had to let go of my ideas of how my life was supposed to be and trust that God's plans for me were greater. The perception of others could no longer be the barometer that I used to gauge my life. My measurements were too small. I wasn't thinking big enough. I was fearfully and wonderfully made, a designer's original sculpted from the Master's hand. I was someone, and it was time that I woke up and walked into my destiny.

Who I am rested in the one who created me, I was God's design. I was unique to Him, and He knew my purpose. The question could only be answered by God; through His word, I would see my reflection. I had to stop wishing that I had a different life. I was abused and rejected. I had had bad relationships. I felt worthless and unloved. This was my reality, and I had to face it in order to move past it.

I began to live on purpose and embrace my story. This was the life God had given me, and through it, the world would see His glory. I am a woman who was denied the love of a father in order to see the love of her Heavenly Father. I was rejected by men in order to understand that He will never leave me. To every action, there was a counteraction that drew me closer to God. My life wasn't an accident; my life became the voice for every little girl whose dreams were stolen. When she would look at my life, she would know that she can live and fulfill her destiny.

> To appoint unto them that mourn in Zion, to give unto them *beauty for ashes*, the oil of joy *for* mourning, the garment of praise *for* the spirit of heaviness; that they might be called trees of righteousness, the planting of the Lord, that he might be glorified (Isa. 61:3, emphasis mine)

My mind had to be reprogrammed to believe that I was more than…whatever negative thoughts that tried to filtrate pass the truth of my existence. I was a child of the King. I had purpose, promises, and privileges.

At a young age, I had become fascinated by the royals. I would watch any program that had kings, queens, and castles. Recently I began watching *Downton Abbey*, a series on PBS. It is a British drama that follows the lives of the Crawley family and its servants as they interact with each other. I was always amazed at the relationship between the two classes. It wasn't just the money that separated them, but rather it was titles. As long as you had a title in front of your name, you were expected to have certain things granted to you.

I took that same concept and applied it to my life; my titles are daughter, friend, beloved, anointed, blessed, favored, and chosen. With those titles, I expect the promises of God to be fulfilled, I expect prayers to be answered, and I expect to be loved.

This is why it is so important to guard your mind. Whenever the devil tries to steal my truth, I plant my feet solid and look into a mirror and say you are fabulous! Your Father is the King of kings. You have worth, and you are loved. I would say this not because of what I have done, but because of who I am in Christ. That alone gives me reassurance, and it takes the weight off me trying to fix things. I was able to put the past behind me simply by reaching for what is in front of me. I can walk in my newness knowing that I am not alone. I always share that I have the greatest posse around. I have the Father who is over me, the Son of God walking beside me, the Holy Spirit within me, His angels encamped around me, and I have the prayers of the righteous. What do I have to fear!

Gradually, I allow the fear I was experiencing to dissipate. I began to open up my heart in order to start living. I allowed people into my life sharing small bits of my heart, soul, and emotions. The first person I allowed into my heart was a woman younger than I. She was quirky and odd. But in her uniqueness, I saw her passion for Christ. She was diligent in building the kingdom of God. I loved her spirit; she was confident in who she was, she walked in her purpose. Her personality drew me in. I wanted to know more. I knew that she wouldn't judge me; she was someone who cared more about the person than the persona. I found strength in her character.

We spent a weekend together at the annual youth retreat. I volunteered to be a chaperone. To be completely honest, I felt way out of my comfort zone. I didn't want anyone to notice my discomfort, so I tucked myself away in the kitchen, hoping no one would see me. Once again, I was the spectator while others were living their lives.

Intensively, I watched how she demonstrated care and concern for each child. She spoke with reassurance. She was free in the Lord.

After she shared the message, the group gathered together for prayer. She gave the instructions for us to stand next to someone and pray. It was powerful to see the young people follow her lead and pray sincerely for the person next to them.

After that, she said, "Ask the Lord who you need to pray for?" The young people walked across the room finding that one person that God laid on their hearts. I was still tucked away in the corner, breathing all this in, when all of a sudden, her husband came to me; he reached out for my hand and began to pray. I was startled by this because I came out of a church culture where single women were shunned if they had the slightest type of contact with married men. Even if you looked like you were going to speak to a married man, you were given the "eye," and it was almost impossible to build friendships with their wives. You had to be married to join that club. I didn't realize how I carried those ideas with me as well as the scares from the abuse. When her husband grabbed my hand, my body stiffened as to say, "I am not a willing participate. It's not my fault." The little girl that I had carried was afraid. Then I began to listen to the words that he was praying for me. My body relaxed, and I was able to receive the tenderness of his heart. His prayer was a beam of light that made me feel secure and demonstrated the love of a father. When I got alone with his wife, I told her what I was feeling, and she wrapped her arms around me and said, "You are my family, you don't have to be afraid." I was among people who I felt were so different than me, yet they allowed me to connect to God on a greater level and feel a oneness that solidify my being.

When I returned to church, I took what I had experienced and began to open up and share my life. No longer did I hide in the shadows. I took a chance and met people. To my surprise, they were willing to share their lives with me. They wanted to build connections that signified the love of God. People from all walks of life came together for one purpose: to give God the glory and love one another.

That freedom brought me to a place where I felt acceptance. My life had become enlarged by the friendships of others. God was filling my emptiness. I remember a day that I was feeling overwhelmed. My insecurities crept back, and I would be tested. It was the church picnic; people from both services came out to fellowship over food and games. I wanted to run when I saw the number of people, but I was determined to stay and conquer this fear. I found a spot under a tree where I tucked myself neatly away. I waited for the perfect opportunity to submerge into an ongoing conversation. I didn't know how to join in. I had been on the outside so long that I felt socially inept. People would walk by and wave, and I returned the gesture with a wave and a smile.

Who was willing to take a chance on me? I continued to watch how everyone was enjoying themselves. I guess in my own way, I was enjoying the day as well, but God always knows just what you need. I took out a book and began to read. I could feel the ground beating, and when I looked up, there was a small army of people approaching. They wanted to talk to me; they wanted me to feel like I belonged. The conversation lasted almost an hour. We talked about our families, the church, and God. What made this conversation so memorable was that the individuals that came to share their hearts with me were deaf. They showed me what the love of God can do when you were willing to open up. They didn't care that I had to muddle through with my limited sign language; they had opened up their hearts and invited me in. Every Sunday, we would continue to meet and communicate the intent of our hearts. They were becoming friends, and they were becoming my family.

God was opening up my eyes little by little to see the manifestation of His glory. If God would have shown me where I would be in comparison to where I was standing, I would have given up before I even started. I couldn't conjure up such thoughts of victory. Just like an old black-and-white film, my life had to be revealed frame by frame. It was in those moments of His glory I was able to see the light of a new life in Christ. There are no chains that His love can't break.

The Life Lesson

The *steps* of a good man are *ordered* by the Lord: and he delighteth in his way. (Ps. 37:23, emphasis mine)

God was orchestrating my life, and as long as I was willing to follow He would be able to get me to my destination.

Life lesson question: Who are you following?

_____

_____

_____

_____

_____

Chapter 14

Is There a Doctor in the House?

Ihad been through years of praying, fasting, and counseling, but I continued to be haunted by my past. I had long spans of time where I was able to live righteously, then without effort, I would fall back into my old ways of living and thinking. Back into another dead-end relationship, I finally went to God, and asked "Why?" Why wasn't I able to keep the life that God was continuously giving me? The truth be known, I hadn't surrendered completely to God. There were still areas of my life that I didn't want to confront; my heart had a Pandora's box. I felt that the darkness that I carried was even too massive for God to heal. Although I was willing to show Him my bandages, I wasn't willing to show him what was underneath.

Spiritually, I was covered in bandages. Instead of allowing God to attend to my wounds, I just covered them with bandages of relationships, isolation, work, and even church. Never attending to the sores of my soul caused an infection that caused my life to stink. I was trying to heal myself instead of going to the one who was able to heal me completely, the Great Physician. Is there a doctor in the house that could attend to my infirmities? Because I didn't realize the depth of my infection. God showed me what would happen if I didn't allow Him to attend to the wounds of my heart. God used natural things to demonstrate things in the spirit.

When my mother's health began to decline, we had to make choices about her overall well-being. We met as a family and decided to divide the responsibilities of her care. One person took care of her finances, another person took care of her doctor appointments, and still another took care of her meals. My responsibilities were to take care of her hygiene, which also included caring for her wounds.

Although my mother lived at home, there were times when she had to receive outside care. While under the care of an outside agency, she received a devastating wound. Once she returned home, her care was elevated. She had visiting nurses that came to take care of her medical needs. Since the nurses could not come every day, I was trained to administer treatment. I would have to remove the old bandages, clean the area, apply medicine, and redress it with new clean bandages. God had shown me that this was a replica of my life. My wounds needed to be attended too.

I had never really let God examine the wounds that I carried. I continuously kept them covered so that others would not see how bad I was hurting. It was okay to show the bandages, but the depth of pain I was feeling was underneath. Just like in the natural, if you don't clean the wounds, you take the risk of becoming infected. I couldn't heal properly because I wasn't willing to uncover the bandages of my life.

I made a choice to allow God to go into the dark places of my soul. Once again, I was put into a vulnerable place, but I wouldn't be alone. I confessed to God that I was broken; I finally was able to share the deep dark secrets of my life. I needed God to reach down in the caverns of my soul. I needed a true healing. The truth had finally set in; I wasn't equipped to fix my own life. I had to go to the one who created me, and knew all about me. He said, "Remove those old bandages."

By unwrapping those feelings of insecurity, worthlessness, hatred, and shame, I would expose what was underneath. Before I could share my life with anyone, I had to be willing to share it with God first. When your wounds are exposed, you take a risk of allowing others to infect you so the doctor will make a decision to keep you isolated from others to limit the risk. For a while, I felt like I was placed in isolation. My contacts were limited to God the Father, God the Son, and the Holy Spirit. If you find yourself in a position of isolation, you might be under the care of the great physician.

He will *cover* you with His feathers, and under his wings you will find refuge; his faithfulness will be your shield and rampart. (Ps. 91:4, NIV; emphasis mine)

Once the bandages were removed, God had to clean the areas of my heart that were soiled by the circumstances of my life, the sins of others, and the sins I committed. There I stood uncovered, waiting for God to cleanse me. It was there I began to imagine myself standing at the foot of the cross, completely open and honest; and when Jesus sees me, He takes the blood from His hands and begins to wash me until I am clean.

But if we walk in the light, as he is in the light, we have fellowship with one another, and the *blood of* **Jesus**, his Son, purifies us from all sin. (1 John 1:7, emphasis mine)

I had gotten used to self-medicating. I used the things of the world to heal the pain I was feeling. I used people as an ointment to bring comfort. Now it was time for me to allow God to prescribe the medication that would bring a complete healing and not a temporary fix. The true medicine was the Word of God. I had to place a heavy dose of His word over every situation in my life. It didn't matter what I was feeling. God had a word of healing.

[*Jesus Heals the Sick*] Jesus went throughout Galilee, teaching in their synagogues, proclaiming the good news of the kingdom, and *healing* every disease and sickness among the people. (Matt. 4:23, emphasis mine)

Finally, I had to apply new bandages. The new bandages came in the form of a renewed mind. I had to apply bandages of faith and hope. I had to change the way I was thinking. Every time I wanted to think like the old me, I pictured me taking those old dirty bandages out of the trash and applying them to my heart. I knew if I did that, I would cause myself to become sick again. A changed mind can change your life.

> Therefore, I urge you, brothers and sisters, in view of God's mercy, to offer your bodies as a living sacrifice, holy and pleasing to God—this is your true and proper worship. Do not conform to the pattern of this world, but be transformed by the renewing of your mind. Then you will be able to test and approve what God's will is—his good, pleasing and perfect will. (Rom. 12:1–3, NIV)

God was doing a great thing in my life; the changes that I tried to make before didn't last because I was trying to do it myself. Once I surrendered to God, I saw an irrefutable change in my life. I was walking into my destiny. The question that caused me so much uncertainty was being answered. I knew my purpose and I knew how to fulfill my purpose. I wasn't someone who experienced an immediate revelation that I was healed. My life had to be filtered through the grace of God in order to receive a complete deliverance.

I have heard a lot of things said in my life, like it's okay for a preacher to hurt just as a long as they don't bleed on the congregation. This made me feel like I couldn't be truthful with the people who wanted to hear the truth. I thought about those who enter a hospital with injuries, oftentimes bleeding from the traumas they have experienced. Does the hospital personnel say, "I see that you are hurting, but I can't help you because you have blood on you"? What they do is get protective gear, gowns, and gloves and attend to the patients. We have the same protective gear that will cover us when we go to help those that are hurting. He's called the Holy Spirit.

The Life Lesson

> He said, "If you will listen carefully to the voice of the *Lord* your God and do what is right in his sight, obeying his commands and keeping all his decrees, then I will not make you suffer any of the diseases I sent on the Egyptians; for I am the *Lord* who heals you." (Exod. 15:26, NLT; emphasis mine)

Obedience in the Lord would bring the healing I needed.

Life lesson question: Do you believe that God can heal you?

_____

_____

_____

_____

_____

_____

_____

_____

Chapter 15

Forgive Yourself

The anger raged strong within me. Yes, I had forgiven God, but I still struggled with my perceptions, and I was unable to forgive myself. The unforgiveness I felt had hindered how I believed God interacted with me. When people would come to me and ask for prayer, I had no doubt that God was going to come through. I believed that God is a healer, a deliverer, and a restorer for anyone who came looking for a miracle. Yes, I believed for everyone, but me.

I know that we were created in the image of God, but when I looked into the mirror of my soul, I didn't see who God saw. I saw the broken, ashamed, and hurt little girl. No matter what I did, I couldn't shake the image of how I saw myself. I needed to see me through the eyes of God. I wanted to see my reflection differently.

God had given me a step-by-step process to follow: four things I would have to do in order to reach my full potential in God. First, I had to *acknowledge* where I was spiritually, then *embrace* the life that I was given, followed by making a *decision* that I was going to change, and finally I would have to *declare* the truth.

I had to *acknowledge* the circumstances of my life. Yes, I was abused; yes, I made bad decisions that had effected how I lived and believed. I had given so much of my life over to the enemy. Acknowledging where I was and what I had endured gave me the ability to take charge of my life. I wasn't the victim that I made my mind to believe. I was much more. I had to change how I thought about the situation. It was no longer going to keep me from the life that God had promised. I found scriptures that gave me the strength. I was able to tuck away the Word of God deep inside my heart, giving me strength to fight for a better life.

> *If* we *confess* our sins, he **is** faithful and just and will forgive us our sins and purify us from all unrighteousness. (1 John 1:9, emphasis mine)
>
> Make allowance for each other's faults, and *forgive* anyone who offends you. Remember, the Lord forgave you, so you must *forgive others*. (Col. 3:13, emphasis mine)

I gave it all to God. I confessed my thoughts and my actions. I had the chance for a do over. I would no longer be concerned about how others perceived me. I wasn't going to worry about the reactions of others if the secrets got out. God has made me righteous. I was going to walk in victory. My life was unfolding into God's plan.

If you want to make God laugh, tell Him your plans. If it was left up to me, my life would have looked differently. There would have been no abuse or rejection. I would have married a king, lived in a castle, and rode away on a white horse. I would have danced in ballets across the country. I would have had a voice that sounded like angels. I would have a fashion sense that could stun the runways. That was wishful thinking but somewhat selfish.

Our lives are supposed to be living epistles, and through the ups and downs of life, we should come closer to Jesus and draw others. I am thankful that God was in control.

I had to *embrace* the pain and suffering I endured, for it has developed my heart to show compassion, forgiveness, and love. I have my life and I celebrated every tear, every heartache, and every bad relationship because it is through the pain and suffering that I have been able to touch others. Embracing my life has given me the courage to speak about what I had endured.

Without any fanfare, God began to position women in my life that had similar stories. I remember one time I was out in a parking lot, looking for the perfect cart, which is impossible, when I casually began a conversation with a woman. It was just the basic stuff, "Hi, how's your day going?" Before I knew it, she was sharing intimate details of her life. That she had been abused and how it affected her life. Only God could bring strangers together and make them feel like friends. This started happening more and more. In the beginning, it felt weird to hear their stories. Total strangers trusting me with the ability to share in their lives. Conversations about shopping or the kids would end with women sharing the hidden things of their hearts. Oftentimes, my ears and heart would be the first to hear their stories. The difference was I truly understood their pain. I was able to listen with compassion. The crowds became larger. I was unaware of the fact that God was preparing me for greater opportunities.

This was my life, and I had to make a *decision*. What would I do with what God has given me?" I made a choice to say yes, and use my life as a testimony of the goodness of God. I was going to wear my scars as badges of honor for the glory of God.

Through this stage in my process, gifts began to unfold and talents revealed. As quickly as I was emptying out, God was filling me up with new strength and power. I am His daughter, and I have purpose. Each one of us has to make a decision whether you will follow God. Will you move past your own insecurities, shame, and guilt to reach the masses?

The final stage in my process was to *declare* the truth. The truth that Jesus shed on the cross. The truth that states that no matter what you go through, if you just trust in God He will work everything out for your good. His love has the ultimate power to transform your life. By declaring the truth, I was truly set free. This is why I continue to speak the Word of God with boldness and authority.

> Then *you will* know the *truth*, and the *truth will set you free*." (John 8:32, emphasis mine)

The Life Lesson

I love watching the movie *Field of Dreams*. One of my favorite lines in it is, "If you build it, they will come." God was building a place of safety and rest within me so that others would find Him. When you say yes to God, He is able to build out of the rubble of your life. When I focused on what had happened to me, my life seemed so small. Once I was able to step out of myself, I was able to see a larger picture. God hadn't forgotten about me, and He hasn't forgotten about you.

> The LORD replies, "I have seen violence done to the helpless, and I have heard the groans of the poor. Now I will rise up to rescue them, as they have longed for me to do." (Ps. 12:5)

Life lesson question: Are you willing to forgive yourself?

_____

_____

_____

_____

_____

Chapter 16

Welcome Home, Daddy!

The abuse had ended, but the view never changed. I could still see my dad's house from my kitchen window. I wondered if he could see me. I grew up hating the man and longing for the father. He was supposed to love me, protect me, and care for me. I always wished that I had been able to experience the love of my father, but as I grew, the hatred grew deeper. I continued the masquerade, not for him but for my own sake. I had lived this lie for so long that I became the lie. Secretly, I would look for any glimmer of hope that would erase those years, anything that would say that I was worthy of a real dad.

Time hadn't been kind to him; the signs that he was aging became evident in his slow steps, his diminishing sight, limited strength, and crumpled hands. I no longer feared the man who once towered over me. He was no longer a threat. My hatred for him was softening by the pity I felt for him. This was my time for revenge, but I couldn't find it within me to cause him any more pain. My father's ailments became worse, and after having several car accidents, he was placed in a nursing home for rehabilitation.

This was my break; I didn't have to see him anymore. I had a choice. He wasn't going to affect my life anymore. I could walk in my neighborhood, walk by his house, and keep walking. It was a sense of relief. Several weeks had passed, and I felt empowered. I had taken control of my life no one was going to make me see him. I was embracing his absence. I thought it was finished. That's what I told myself.

While at work, I decided to decorate a bulletin board. It was my time to be creative and inspiring. The theme would be "dream big." As I was placing the colorful backdrop, I felt a strong breeze push pass me. I turned to see if someone had left the side door open, but it was closed tightly. I continued to work, although I was feeling uneasy, as if I wasn't alone. I took a moment to quiet myself, remembering God's words, "Be still, and know that I am God" (Ps 46:10). I stapled the background paper up, I felt God say, "It's time, go see him."

I have felt God speaking to me before, but this time, it couldn't be God. He knew what I had endured at the hands of my father. He knew the freedom that I was finally feeling. Why would he want to reopen those wounds? Still I heard, "Go see him!" I was overwhelmed with an urgency that I couldn't explain, I thought it was finished.

For me, it was out of sight, out of mind. The end of the day came quickly. I jumped into my car, hoping that it would automatically drive me home, bypassing the nursing home. I couldn't shake the feeling I had to go. I was torn between being obedient and maintaining my sense of freedom. Obedience won!

Once I reached the stop sign, I struggled to make a right turn. I continued to question God's voice. The sound of an annoyed driver brought me back to the reality I was facing. I threw my hand up and made a quick right turn. The speed limit was 35 mph, but if I drove at 10 mph, maybe the visiting hours would be over. What should have taken five minutes took me twenty minutes, but I finally reached the nursing home.

I sat in the parking lot, trying to figure out why I was there, what I would say, and how I should feel. I was able to grasp a few ounces of courage that pushed me through the front doors and up to his room. I stood in the doorway holding my breath. Maybe this was a test. I just had to go there and seeing him wasn't a requirement. I silently yelled, "GOD WHAT DO YOU WANT FROM ME?"

As I turned to run out of the building, I heard my father ask the nurse, "Was somebody here?" I ducked tightly against the wall in hopes that she didn't see me, but I was too late. The nurse spotted me as she walked out of the room. "Yes, there is a young lady here." She told me, "Okay you can go in now."

I slowly walked to his bedside as flashes of the past flooded my mind. I counted my steps, wondering if it was the same number of steps I had to walk to go into his house. As I turned to look at my father, this fragile man humbled himself and spoke these words; "I am sorry for everything I ever did to you."

Right at that moment, the hatred that I carried for him lifted. The weight was off, and I was truly renewed. I had a daddy, I had my daddy. God knew exactly what I needed, and by blessing me, He also blessed my dad.

I visited him every day from that moment on, and nobody told me I had to go. We would spend hours talking, filling those empty pots of our past with new memories that could grow. One of my greatest memories I have with my dad was the day when I was able to pray with him. Not only did he ask me for forgiveness, he also asked Jesus for forgiveness. To hear his fragile voice become strong when he said, "I want Jesus Christ as my Savior" caused me to see a different man, I saw my dad. What an awesome God we serve.

A few weeks later, my father died from complications the results of hip surgery. I can't imagine how I would have felt if I chose not to listen to the voice of God. Forgiving my father snatched the pain away. The heaviness my heart felt was replaced with wings that allowed my heart to soar beyond the barriers of my past. I was free, truly free.

The Life Lesson

I always wanted to have a relationship with my father. I used to deny the fact that I needed to have that relationship restored. I thought that if I just walked away and acted like he didn't exist that those feelings would go away. God knew just what I needed to heal.

This is your moment to get involved. Take a moment and think about that one thing that has hindered you from moving forward. You got it? Now give it to God and tell Him to restore, remove, or refresh that thought in order for you to get to a place of healing. God hasn't forgotten you. He's just waiting for you to yield your heart and mind over to him. Let's take a ride on the potter's wheel.

Life lesson question: Are you willing to get on the Potter's wheel?

_____

_____

_____

_____

_____

_____

_____

_____

_____

_____

_____

_____

Chapter 17

My Past Was Buried

I had learned that forgiveness had the power to set me free. The one person who I hated the most was my cousin. There was still a small part of me that believed that he was the catalyst that propelled me into my life of destruction. Those roots of anger ran deep within my heart. After the last encounter with him, I wasn't sure if I was even strong enough to be in his proximity, but I would find out today.

A family member had passed away, and as usual, my mother and I were the representatives, and she made sure we were in attendance. It seems that weddings and funerals were the only times we got together as a family.

We went to church and arrived early so that I could park near the entrance; by now, it was becoming more difficult to get Mom around. My focus was on getting her situated and finding her a seat. She liked to sit at the end of the row and near the back of the church. This meant that we had to arrive early to get her special spot.

The church was so quiet. I swore everyone could hear my heart racing, sounding like African tribal drums preparing for war. We found our seat and listened to the stream of witnesses that sung and spoke on the behalf of the deceased. Speeches so moving that you wanted the person to rise up and hear the accolades. I was surprised because to look at the person, you may have wondered if you were at the correct funeral.

My thoughts began to drift wondering if my life had made an impact on the world as they had accomplished. What would be spoken of me? Who would show up? Did I make my mark in the world? Funerals have a way of making you look into your own life and question your very existence.

The service turned out to be a beautiful home-going. The pastor gave the signal for the funeral director to get into position so that they could take over, and we could transition to the grave site. I made it through round one without any hits. I followed the procession with flashing lights, hoping that once we arrived, I would be able to position the car in such a way that my mom would be able to see the service without having to get out of the car. Perfect. I found the spot so that she could see and hear the service without having to maneuver through the dirt and over the numerous plots.

I got out of the car and walked over to the grave site. I stood by the clergy so that I could fill my official duties, but I also stood by them just in case things got ugly. I was trusting that they would keep the service in order. One wrong move, and it might have been a pileup on top of the casket. The service went without any disruptions. Everyone did their part. I must say it was a good service, and even nicer that we were able to come together as a family, a real family.

I saw my cousin from the corner of my eye. I felt my body becoming tense; the little girl that God had set free was standing locked in fear. The voice of God spoke to me and said, "Go to him." I thought God was asking a lot from me. I wasn't the same little girl. I was older, and I had watched enough karate movies that I was ready to kick butt (if only in my mind).

I obeyed. I picked up one foot then another, walking slowly at first; but with each step, I felt a strength stirring within me. When I reached him, he was engaged in a conversation, so I waited. I could see that when he was ending the conversation, he had planned to go in another direction, so I gently grabbed his hand. I wasn't afraid. He turned and looked at me and asked the question, "Who are you?"

I wanted to say, "I am the little girl who trusted you, and believed in you, but you took that trust and exploited my innocence for your pleasures. Yes, I am that little girl who hasn't been able to maintain a stable relationship, felt worthless, and even at times turned my back on God. You don't remember me? Is that because there were so many others that I wasn't a person just an object of your distorted mind." But I couldn't; something was different. I told him my name, and he said, "You don't look the same."

Those five small words gave confirmation that God had completed a divine makeover. I wasn't the same little girl. God took that situation and turned it around for my good.

At a funeral, standing in the midst of death, I was able to forgive my cousin. I drove out of the graveyard, knowing that there was one more thing that was buried there, my past.

If anyone would have known of the horrible act that had taken place between my cousin and me, they couldn't see it that day. I made peace with the man I hated for so long. At the repast, we sat together, we ate together, and we even laughed together.

I can't say that this will be the story for everyone. You may be able to forgive, but not in a position to be around the person who hurt you. That's okay. God will only give you what you need and what you can handle.

God knew for me, I needed closure. I needed to feel that I had overcome, and I was empowered. The little girl that was so afraid doesn't have to be afraid anymore.

God is still amazing me that when things seem impossible, God's grace makes them possible. Since the funeral, I have seen my cousin a few times, and each time we embrace by the love of God. So for me, it is finally finished.

The Life Lesson

Maybe it's not always trying to fix something broken. Maybe it's about starting over and creating something better.

It was time for me to stop trying to fix the problem. It was time that I allow God to give me the opportunity to start my life anew. Better was waiting for me.

Life lesson question: Are you ready to bury your past?

_____

_____

_____

_____

_____

_____

_____

_____

Chapter 18

A Rescue to Restoration

Here is a rescue to restoration story. The commander yelled, "Cease fire." It was one of his longest battles he had endured. It had been over three decades since the war began, and the opposing soldiers weren't letting up. What was so special about this one captured soldier that they were willing to risk everything they had to save her life? The commander's soldiers began to murmur among themselves and questioned why he ordered a cease fire. He heard their concerns and replied, "We sent out our best soldiers, and every one of them were defeated. I sent out fornication, and he was subdued by purity, then I sent out worthlessness, and he was shot down by confidence and courage. It didn't matter what soldier I sent out, there was always someone there to defeat them, and what I don't understand is that there were only three on the front line. We just need to release the prisoner and find someone else."

God was unrelenting in His pursuit for me. He was willing to fight for me, and even though it looked like there was severe casualities, He continued to fight.

The captured soldier was taken to the medics where she was given a blood transfusion. As the bag of blood slowly dripped into her spirit, she was refreshed, renewed, and restored. Once healed, that soldier went back on the battlefield to fight for other captured soldiers.

The difference was this soldier realized that the battle was already won, so she didn't have to fight for the victory because she was fighting with victory. God's love is persistent. He will continually go after you so that you will be the person that fulfills the destiny He has placed within you.

I still remember all the painful memories, but I am no longer affected by them. I am not moved in my thoughts or actions by what has happened to me. I have learned to use them as a platform to share the redeeming love of Jesus Christ. This isn't the end to my story but rather I have been given the chance to begin again. I couldn't do this on my own. I wasn't strong enough, but I could do it through the power and strength of Jesus Christ.

With a renewed mind, I was able to experience a fullness that came from God. It doesn't matter if it's been two days or twenty years. You still have a chance to get the life you were promised to receive. If God hasn't given up on you, then you shouldn't give up on yourself. My life took a series of turns and detours, but the journey was worth the destination. God is calling you back home.

God was able to bring me to a place of restoration. He restored the joy of my salvation, He restored my peace, and He restored my love.

> But as it is written, Eye hath not seen, nor ear heard, neither have entered into the heart of man, the things which God hath prepared for them that love him.
> —1 Corinthians 2:9 (KJV)

One of the greatest fears I had was changed. I had lived in the shadows of my abuse so long that I didn't know any other way to live. I was a prisoner in my own mind. The doors were open, and God was calling me to come out. The sound of his voice was reassuring, but still I hesitated. I tried to imagine what my life was going to look like, and it overwhelmed me.

Step by step, I began to walk into my destiny. I opened my heart to love the way God intended. No longer do I have a distorted view. I know what real love looks like, and it is truly beautiful. I found courage that I didn't know existed. In God's sight, not a moment was wasted; no matter what I went through, He continues to prune until

I become what He created me to be. Once I completely surrendered to Him., He was able to restore my life. I have no regrets.

You may question what my life looks like now—it's victorious. Since I have embedded my life in Christ, I am able to live my best life now. Yes, I still have problems and situations that arise, but I have a Savior who is more than able to work on my behalf. Gospel recording artist Marvin Sapp said it best in his song "Never Would Have Made It":

I would have lost my mind a long time ago,

If it had not been for you

I am stronger, I am stronger

I am wiser, I am wiser

Now I am better, I am better

So much better, I am better

I am not the woman I once was, I am better. God was able to return a life of grace to me.

I remember the day that I really felt the freedom of God. I was asked to participate in a Fourth of July parade. I thought that it would be fun, so I signed up to walk with the church. On the day of the parade, it began to rain. I should tell you that one of my pet peeves is to have on wet clothes, so standing in the rain wasn't what I had in mind. How in the world was I going to keep smiling when I was so irritated with the rain? I didn't share my disappointments with anyone. (I didn't want to rain on anyone's parade, ha-ha-ha!) When I looked around, the people from my church were all smiles; the rain didn't bother them. As we were walking, the Spirit of the Lord became apparent. I took off the jacket, the rain scarf, and put down the umbrella. I allowed the rain to hit my face and run down my cheeks. I felt it through my entire body. It cooled my soul. This is what freedom feels like, and I was free. I finished the parade with a huge smile. I still don't like wearing wet clothes, but I don't let it affect my joy. From that day on, I made a decision to embrace each day with gladness.

The happiness that I felt transcended to every area of my life. For years, I was unable to see what others saw in me because I believed that my perception reflected how others saw me. I was finally loving myself, and I welcomed the love of others. I made a statement in chapter 11 that I was torn about the decision to leave. I had spent seventeen years with this church, and although I didn't feel loved, I knew that there were people there who loved me. My statement has changed since then; now, I can say, there are people who love me, and I feel their love. Whenever I visit my former church, it feels like home. No longer do I feel like a stranger living on the outside.

There are many reasons why I celebrate. I am grateful for His love that has brought me to a place of salvation. Through his blood, I've been washed and made whole. I've been given another chance, or should I say many chances to get it right. I am overwhelmed by His grace that covers me. I find joy and strength in His arms. He has given me courage that can cast away fear. I could go on and on, but the one thing that continues to humble me is the fact that through it all, God has restored me.

This is why it's *"never too late to cry, for the little girl in the red dress."* You can find what you are looking for when you make a choice to see it through God's plan for your life.

I have been given the awesome task of sharing what He has done for me and what He will do for you. Second Peter 1:3 has become one of my life's scriptures. "By His divine power, God has given us everything we need for a godly life. We have received all of this by coming to know him, the one who called us to himself by means of his marvelous glory and excellence." Grabbing hold of His word has made the transformation possible.

The Life Lesson

I surrendered all to God, I became like a child vulnerable to His mercy. I allowed Him to do the work. He took me and reconstructed me into the woman He designed me to be. He gave me even more than I could ever imagine. His love overflowing.

> The Lord rewarded me for doing right; he *restored* me because of my innocence. (Ps. 18:20, emphasis mine)

Life lesson question: Are you in a place to recognize the restoration of God?

_____

_____

_____

_____

_____

_____

_____

Chapter 19

He Saw What I Could Become

For a long time, I lived my life in a whirlwind of my sins. I wasn't able to obtain secure footing because I didn't allow myself to be anchored in God. I let the uncertainties of my emotions lead me. It had become so easy to get immersed in negative thoughts, which catapulted me into a life of destructions. I had taught myself that my life had no worth because of the things that I had suffered, but God! He was able to gather all the pieces of my life; not one was lost. The pieces that were stolen and pieces that I gave away were all gathered in the Master's hand. He didn't look at what I was; He saw what He had created within me.

I am not the same anymore! You might question the sincerity of that statement. What is so different this time, what gives me the confidence that my life has turned around? I am glad you asked. The reason why I know that things have permanently changed in my life is *accountability*.

Earlier this year, I was asked to speak at a Women's Conference in Ocean City. The theme was "Lioness Arising." As I was studying the material and preparing my notes, the voice of God returned. "Tell your story."

I felt there was no need to bring up old news. Wasn't it enough that God had cleansed me and restored me? This was a private act between me and my God. My thoughts were, "Let's move on." I was halfway through writing my sermon when I heard the request again, "Tell your story."

My response was, "Okay, God, I know that our relationship is back in good standing, but are you for real!"

Have you ever poured out liquid from a glass, put it back on the table, only to realize that there is still a few drops left in it? That was God and me. Although He had emptied me out, He wanted me to know that there were still a few more drops that needed to go. By telling my story, I would finally empty out all of the shame and guilt that I carried. The secrets could no longer hold me hostage. I wrestled with the thought and was ready to keep my drops in order to preserve my perceived integrity.

As I was walking to the area where I would be presenting, I felt an overwhelming presence of the Holy Spirit. The hallway was thick with a fog that seemed to have no origin.

As I moved through the fog, I heard a sound that was indescribable; but it made me believe that heaven had opened up, and God Himself was going to be in the attendance. It was the scripture manifest: "For where two or three are gathered together in my name, there am I in the midst of them" (Matt. 18:20). There were a few ladies at the end of the hall praying for the conference and praying on my behalf. I still didn't know if I would have the courage to share my story.

Once the praise and worship had ended, it was my turn to speak. I stood in front of a room full of women. I saw them collectively waiting to hear from the Lord. I looked at my notes and began sharing, when all of a sudden, I began to see the women individually. I saw faces covered in tears, I saw hearts yearning for hope, I saw women, and I saw my sisters.

I continued to reflect from the notes I had written until I got to the same spot where I heard the voice of God earlier. I heard God's voice clearly again, "Tell your story."

I put the notes down and opened my mouth and I allowed God to speak through me. When I had finished sharing, I believe that God had given me a standing ovation for my obedience. I was His daughter, and He was well pleased.

One of the things I shared was that God had given me a gift to recognize those who had been through what I had been through.

I call it a "me too" spirit. As the women came to hug me and say thank-you, there were some who whispered, "Me too."

Once I hugged my last sister, I walked back over to the pulpit and told them what God had required of me: to write my story. I asked the women to hold me accountable, and they agreed. I wasn't alone anymore. I had a tribe of believers holding me up to live the life that God had promised me.

When I do anything, I have to think about how it will reflect on those who have been a banner for me. Light was hitting me from all directions, and everyone knows that darkness can't hide in the light. I am grateful for the encouragement that I receive from every woman that takes time out to see me.

I remember being in church, and it was the altar call. This was a pivotal part of worship. The pastor finished his sermon and began beckoning to the congregation to open up their hearts to receive Jesus Christ. With bowed heads and a few peeking eyes, people began to walk to the altar, looking for a way out of their troubles. I spotted a man that lived in the neighborhood. His life had taken an awful turn. He was on the verge of allowing life's circumstances to swallow him up. I was excited to see that he wasn't going to give up and that he had made a choice to try Jesus. The next Sunday came, and there he was again sobbing at the altar. What could have happened that brought him back again. For the next seven weeks, I witnessed this man make the same walk up front to receive Jesus Christ. After a few times, you could hear the whispers, "Here he goes again." Those are the whispers that kept me and so many others from continuing to fight. Maybe if I would have kept making that walk, someone would have noticed that I was struggling; but like so many people, we refused to be exposed, fearing what others will think of us. Keep coming until the change you need sticks.

The Life Lesson

She has been rummaging through the trash trying to find her treasures that were lost through the decisions of life. She was once crowned a queen, now living as a pauper. She knows that if anyone sees her, the whispers will begin, and her character would be in question. She has become what she feared. She could only find comfort among those who are broken too. They didn't see her; they only saw what they could get from her. They don't want her; they only want what she is able to give them. She waits until the coast is clear and ventures out one more time to look for her jewels. She knows once they are returned, the queen that she is will be revealed. I spent my days looking for that one thing that would change my life. I wanted to find love, so that I could be loved. I found what I was looking for when I saw the one who was able to see me, JESUS! If He did it for me, then He will do it for you.

> Many Samaritans from the village believed in Jesus because the woman had said, "He told me everything I ever did!" When they came out to see him, they begged him to stay in their village. So he stayed for two days, long enough for many more to hear his message and believe. Then they said to the woman, "Now we believe, not just because of what you told us, but because we have heard him ourselves. Now we know that he is indeed the Savior of the world." (John 4:39–42)

Life lesson question: Mirror, mirror on the wall . . . What do you see when you look into the mirror of your soul?

_____

_____

_____

_____

_____

_____

_____

_____

_____

_____

_____

_____

_____

Chapter 20

It Was Only the Beginning

One letter, one word, and one sentence, the story of my life was unfolding. The little girl in the red dress has grown up to be a woman of God who is grateful for the journey. The lessons I have learned helped me to embrace the truth that I am "More than a conqueror" (Rom. 8:37). Most stories have an ending, but I refuse to say that this is the end of my story. This is only the beginning of what God has prepared for me. His gifting has stretched me, taking me to places I never thought I would go, giving me experiences I never dreamed of; and giving me a podium to share the Glory of God. How awesome!

People have asked me if I have any regrets or if given the chance, would I have change my life? And I simply say, "No." God knows every detail of my life, and He has prepared me to be victorious. His promises still remain true. The emphasis shouldn't focus on how you began, but the emphasis should rest on how you finish.

The story of my life continues with a greater understanding of who I am. I have purpose and destiny. Through this book, I was able to release everything that held me hostage. I AM FREE!

> If the Son therefore shall make you free, ye shall be free indeed. (John 8:36)

I almost forgot to tell you that the one reason I couldn't get an answer to my question, "What is my purpose?" was that I was asking the wrong question. It should have been "How do I fulfill my purpose?" As a child of God, we all have a purpose to draw others to Christ. God equips us with gifts and talents. God was showing me my entire life how to live in my destiny, and how to fulfill my purpose.

Piece by piece, my life was returned to me through the acts of forgiveness, trust, and love. I was made whole again. I became transparent in order to share the greatest story ever told, the amazing love of God. The world's view on love has been distorted. Many people have similar stories of being abused, rejected, and abandoned, but their stories didn't have a happily ever after or a pot of gold at the end of the rainbow. I wrote this for them and those who have yet to find their destiny.

As I was writing, I saw two different cases where little girls were abused. The first girl was raped by her mother's boyfriend, and the other little girl was sold by her mother for heroin. Not only did I cry for the little girls, I cried for the mothers who weren't able to see beyond their pain and see themselves with value. They had the power to be the reflection of strength, power, and love that their children could become. These mothers didn't figure out the power and influence they have to make a difference in the lives of their children and in the world.

We all have the power to reach someone, and this is my lifeline to someone calling them to safety. God is calling us back home; He wants to reset our lives. Peace and comfort are waiting for you. Your story isn't the ending, but it's the beginning of something greater. What the world sees as broken, God sees as a work of art. You have great value! Whatever has stopped you from living, go back and claim your life. Go back and get what the devil stole from you. It's not too late.

A mother bird will take her babies and toss them out of the nest. If they begin to fall, she will catch them, return them to the safety of the nest, and try again until her babies realize that they are birds, and birds fly. Do you know who you are? You are more than what you have been through, it's time that you fly.

My mother was a woman of few words. She wasn't a person who joined auxiliaries or charities. Her name didn't hang in lights, but what she did was use her gift of cooking to bless a community; her cooking represented her love for God. I grew up watching many people be blessed by this simple act of kindness. I learned a lot from my mother when she said, "Use what you have, and God will do the rest." I pray that my love of writing brings you to a place of healing, where you can find the courage to tell your story, and use what you have!

God will allow us to go through difficult moments in order to show us what's inside of us. My desire is to help every woman find their true value in Christ. We are so much more than what has happened to us. I want everyone that reads this book to examine their lives and see the miracle that God has in you. If we were to sit together and be real for once, we would find out that we are more alike than different. We all have a story to tell and we all have a helping hand to offer. Let us come together so that the next generation won't be afraid to live their stories, of power, hope, and love.

The Life Lesson

I welcomed the newness that God had given me, through the sacrifice of the cross, the power of His resurrection, and the hope of His glory. I am so glad that I don't look like what I had been through. God has given me a spiritual makeover.

Therefore, if any man be in Christ, he is a new creature: old things are passed away; behold, all things are become new. (2 Cor. 5:17)

Life lesson question: Can you see the new you in Christ?

_____

_____

_____

_____

_____

_____

_____

_____

_____

_____

_____

_____

_____

Chapter 21

Tell Your Story

This last section of the book is solely for you. Everyone has a story to tell, and whether you decide to write a book, sing it in a song, paint a picture, or declare it on the street corner, you are free, you are blessed, and you are healed. Satan wants us to believe that no one will understand what we have been through, but there are more. If we were to come together and support one another, we would have incredible strength. Just like chain links, the more you put together, the stronger the chain will become. Find that person that you can link up with that will give you strength. So that you can give strength to others.

> He *comforts* us in all our troubles so that we can *comfort others*. When they are troubled, we will be able to give them the same *comfort* God has given us. (2 Cor. 1:4, emphasis mine)

Your platform may be your neighborhood, community, world, or your kitchen table—it doesn't matter as long as you are willing to share the voice that God has given you. Don't take the voice of someone else and measure your life to theirs; be the best self you can be.

This Is Your Story

_____

_____

_____

_____

_____

_____

_____

_____

_____

_____

_____

_____

_____

_____

For those of you who haven't accepted Jesus Christ as your Savior, take a few moments and ask Him to come into your heart, ask Him to forgive you, save you, and deliver you. This simple act of obedience will line the path of your life with the signs to get you to your destiny. Jesus is waiting for you to come. I guarantee that your life will be the best life once you give it to Jesus Christ.

Prayer

Heavenly Father, thank You for loving me through the messes of my life. I ask You to come into my heart. I surrender every part of who I am to be like You. You have healed and restored me back to a place of love and safety. I completely give my heart, mind, and body to You so that you can make and mold me. I want to be clay in Your hands. Take every piece of my life and form me into the person You created. I want the world to see Your love, Your grace, and Your mercy. Give me the strength and authority in order to win the fight. Lord, continue to show me that I don't have to fight for victory, because I have You in my life, I now fight with victory. I will continue to share of Your goodness, so that others will recognize You as Savior and Lord. In Jesus's name. Amen.

Life Lesson Questions

1. What has pulled you away from the safety of your Heavenly Father?
2. Do you realize who caused the pain in your life?
3. What has God done for you already? Make a list.
4. How do you see your life, and are you magnifying your problems?
5. Where are you placing your affections?
6. What voices are you allowing to give you directions?
7. What are you hiding behind, what are you using to medicate your problem?
8. What and who are you trusting?
9. Whose keeping you company?
10. What lessons are you learning from your issues?
11. Do you really want to change?
12. Do you believe that you are worth changing?
13. Who are you following?
14. Do you believe that God can heal you?
15. Are you willing to forgive yourself?
16. Are you willing to get on the Potter's wheel?
17. Are you ready to bury your past?
18. Are you in a place to recognize the restoration of God?
19. What do you see when you look into the mirror of your soul?
20. Can you see the new you in Christ?

Thank you

- First, I want to thank God for entrusting me to share my story with the world. I pray that I did it justice.
- To the Cumberland County Workforce Development Staff for pushing me to be more.
- To Rev. Dr. James Dunkins and the Shiloh Baptist Church, "One family" in two locations for teaching me the depth of God's Word.
- To Pastors Ralph and Maria Siegel and the Victory Assembly of God Church for showing me the freedom in the Word of God.
- A special thanks to Jessica Hartwell for the countless hours we sat together sharing ideals and dreams; you kept me believing in the impossible.
- To my team of first readers, who kept it real with me, allowing me to empty every drop: M. Douglas, C. Mckelvey, J. Nazario, S. Joynes, G. Quionas, and M. Sawyer.
- To Ken and Cheryl Mckelvey, for your consistent prayers that kept me afloat. You are the godparents that every little girl would want.
- To Makema Douglas, for showing me it can be done and encouraging me along the way and for reminding me that if you listen, God will speak.
- To my siblings who love me through all my messes and still love me.
- To the memory of my mother who carried me to church, until I was able to walk on my own. Forever grateful for you teaching me about Jesus.
- Last by not least to my son, Tyler, who is still a Godsend. I love you more than I could ever express you are the legacy of my destiny.

About the Author

Essie L. Allen is driven and inspired to help women walk out their purpose and destiny. She is a minister of the gospel who has found strength in being vulnerable and transparent when sharing the Word of God. Through her words, she uses her voice to share about God's love, grace, and restoring power. In sharing her very private, dark, and most personal experiences, she resounds with triumphant through the redemptive power of the Lord. She teaches and encourages with a passion for the hearts of women to be free and alive despite their circumstances. She continues to be grateful, thankful, and joyful for the grace that God has given to her. Her life is a reflection of God's ability to restore the broken. His never-ending grace is obvious in her life.

Essie is the mother of one son, who continues to be her legacy.

CPSIA information can be obtained
at www.ICGtesting.com
Printed in the USA
FFOW03n1832151117
43564285-42341FF